WHAT IS A CHRISTIAN?

WHAT IS
A CHRISTIAN?

(Sermons on the Christian Life)

by

A. LEONARD GRIFFITH

ABINGDON PRESS

NEW YORK · NASHVILLE

Most of the Scripture quotations in this book
are from the Revised Standard Version of the Bible
and are copyright 1946, 1952 *by*
the Division of Christian Education
of the National Council of the
Churches of Christ in the U.S.A.

PRINTED IN GREAT BRITAIN
BY EBENEZER BAYLIS AND SON, LTD.,
THE TRINITY PRESS, WORCESTER, AND LONDON

DEDICATED
TO
MERELIE, MY WIFE

Contents

Foreword

I feel proud to be invited to write a short foreword to this volume of Sermons. In all the upheaval of leaving the City Temple, after my own ministry of almost a quarter of a century, the experience that made me most happy was the assurance that it would be continued by my distinguished successor, Leonard Griffith.

Though our outlook may differ and our emphasis vary, I felt at once a kinship of spirit which deepens as the days pass. The author of this book has become my very dear friend.

These sermons need no recommendation from me. There is not a dull one in the whole volume. I have heard Mr. Griffith preach and, of course, when his vivid and forceful personality is added, the impact of his message is even greater. At the same time, such is his power over words, his skilful choice of them and his brilliant arrangement of his ideas, that a minimum of effect is lost when they are read. The author's wide reading, spiritual insight, and his power to focus the great truths of the Christian religion on to the problems of the modern man are revealed on every page of this most helpful and inspiring volume.

Preaching will not become an effete art while sermons like these are offered to the world. I recommend this book unreservedly and hope it will have the wide circulation it deserves.

LESLIE D. WEATHERHEAD
Minister-Emeritus,
The City Temple,
London.

I

WHAT IS A CHRISTIAN?

"And Jesus said to them, 'Follow me!' " (St. Mark 1:17)

"WHAT IS a Christian?" A friend asked me that question in all seriousness and he wanted a serious answer. We had been talking about spiritual matters when suddenly he brought the conversation down to earth by saying, "What is a Christian? How do I know if I am a Christian?" He felt, as I did, that so many of the loose meanings which we commonly attach to the word are neither adequate nor accurate. Is a man a Christian simply by virtue of not being a Muslim or a Buddhist or a Jew? If so, a hardened criminal might justifiably wear the Christian label. Is he a Christian simply because he lives according to the Golden Rule? Any decent and respectable agnostic may fulfil that condition. Is he a Christian because he belongs to a church and recites the Apostles' Creed? These things he may do and still break the Ten Commandments.

What is a Christian? To find an answer we must go back to the beginning and we must remember that when Jesus walked beside the Sea of Galilee there was not another Christian in the whole world. Peter, Andrew, James and John were good men who feared God and kept the law, but neither they, nor any human beings who lived on this planet before them, could properly be called Christians. These four fishermen became Christians only on a day when Jesus said, "Follow me!" "and they forsook their nets and followed him."

So we have our answer. A Christian is someone who responds to the call of Christ. First and always Christianity is a relationship to a Person. In that sense it differs from great world religions like Judaism and Hinduism, and it differs from Communism and the other rival secular faiths that compete for men's allegiance today. All these direct our loyalty to a theological system, a code of ethics, a philosophy or an ideology, but Christianity alone directs our loyalty to a Person. Where Christ is, there is Christianity, and the Christian is a person who tries to be a follower of Jesus Christ.

We say "tries" because no one succeeds perfectly. How very wrong to assume that either you must be a first-class Christian or else you have no right to call yourself a Christian at all. We should never adopt that attitude toward other things. We do not deny ourselves the privilege of education simply because we are not first-class scholars, or the pleasure of singing because we are not of concert calibre, or the enjoyment of knocking a golf ball because we lack professional skill. Why have people a pathological fear of muffing their Christianity? The real zest in life lies not in achievement but in effort, not in having arrived, but in striving. The Apostle Paul confessed miserable failure in the Christian life. Quite frankly he wrote to the Philippians, "Brethren, I do not count myself to have succeeded . . ." "But," he added, "I press on . . ." That's what it means to be a Christian—not that we should follow Christ perfectly, but that we should follow him at all. It is by virtue of our relationship to Christ that we can call ourselves Christians, and from the very beginning that relationship has meant at least five things; compare it to a star with five points of equal length and equal importance.

I

There is first a *doctrinal* relationship to Christ. It is reasonable, surely, that before we follow any person, before we trust what he has to say and commit our lives to his keeping, we must hold certain convictions about him, decide who and what he is. For nineteen centuries the Church has believed that Jesus of Nazareth, while fully and completely human, revealed in his person, as nothing before or since has ever revealed, the whole nature of God. We have tried to express that truth by calling him the Son of God. We are all created sons of God, but Christ is the only begotten Son, whose earthly character alone bears perfectly the lineaments of the Father in heaven. That is why men have followed Jesus and called him Master and Lord, not because he was the cleverest or bravest man who ever lived, but because he had something different about him, something more than human, something Divine.

Let me tell you about two men. First, a contemporary and friend of mine named Charles Templeton, one of the most attractive and brilliant personalities in Canadian television. Until three years ago he was a minister, an evangelist of tremendous power and influence. You can imagine how the popular magazines have made capital on his return to secular life. Asked why he left the ministry, he invariably replies, "I ceased to believe in the Divinity of Jesus"; and if this did actually happen to his thinking, then we have to respect him, because the preacher who ceases to believe in the Divinity of Jesus has nothing more to preach. The foundations beneath his Gospel have collapsed; he no longer has a Gospel, and if he wants to be honest with himself, he has no alternative but to leave the ministry and earn his living in some secular profession. In spite of intellectual reservations a man may lead a life controlled by the highest Christian principles, but he is still not a Christian if he rejects that fundamental belief which, unless it be true, turns Jesus himself into a liar, makes fiction of the New Testament and reduces nineteen centuries of Christianity to a colossal hoax.

The second man is also a friend of mine, and I am honoured to count him as such, because at the age of eighty-five he radiates the serenity and the glory of a lifetime of comradeship with Christ. He is the Very Rev. Dr. George Pidgeon, the first Moderator of the United Church of Canada, brilliant scholar, Church statesman and saintly Christian. A year ago he wrote this personal testimony for a Canadian newspaper:

"I can accept gratefully the beautiful things said about Jesus, the Man of Galilee, by Unitarians and Jews of our time, and feel at the same time that they leave the question of the person of Jesus still unanswered.

"To me, Jesus, the Christ, is the Eternal Son of God on whom personally I depend for salvation. To me he is a personal presence more real and commanding than any authority on earth, whom I have followed and obeyed through a long career of Christian ministry.

"No experience of the past is clearer than the one in which he came to me and called me to follow him in a life of sacrificial service, and no conviction is stronger than that he will come for me when his use of me here is done."

Our discipleship begins, therefore, with an affirmation of belief, the very conviction reached by the Galilean fishermen in their comradeship with Jesus. Peter articulated it: "Thou art the Christ, the Son of the living God". Difficulties lie in the way of that belief, but difficulties may be overcome if we try to overcome them; and remember that a Christian is a man who *tries* to be a follower of Jesus Christ. He does not pretend to be sure where he is not sure, but he does look at Jesus hard enough and close enough and long enough, until he can say with a great sceptic, "I must believe in you. Your life is the highest I know. I cannot call the highest I know a lie. I must call the highest I know the truth. But that means that the eternal is like you. Behind the externalities of this strange universe is a spirit, the truth about which we know when we see you. Lord, I believe. Help thou mine unbelief!"

II

To be a Christian means also a *redemptive* relationship to Christ. At this point of the star Christianity becomes just a little fuzzy for some of us, difficult to understand and certainly difficult to articulate. What do people mean when they speak lovingly and tenderly about Jesus Christ as their Redeemer and Saviour? This rather mystical and intimate language pervades the writings of St. Paul, and there is no understanding of Paul apart from it. "I live, yet not I, but Christ liveth in me. . . . I count everything but loss for the excellency of the knowledge of Christ Jesus my Lord. . . .

In my flesh I complete what is lacking in Christ's afflictions for the sake of his body. . . ." Paul was a man in Christ, a man completely surrendered to Christ. There was nothing that Paul would not do for Christ, because Paul believed that Christ had done everything for him. Just as surely as if someone had snatched him from a blazing inferno, so Christ had redeemed him from the hell of moral futility, sterile Pharisaism and misguided passion and made him a new creature at peace with himself, with his fellow men and with God. From first to last the writings of this great apostle are a song of praise exalting the all-sufficient Saviourhood of Christ.

In becoming a follower of Jesus, the great question is not what we can do for him, but rather what we are willing that he should do for us. There is a story about a minister who went to the home of an old lady with a sum of money to help her pay the rent. He knocked several times at the door, but no one answered, so he left with the gift still in his possession. It turned out that the old lady had been in all the time, and her explanation was, "I heard the knocking, but I thought it was my landlord come to ask for the rent." It is no landlord who knocks on the doors of our hearts, but a Friend, and he brings not a demand, but a gift. Because he is God's Incarnate Son, he brings us the power of God unto salvation; and to open the door and accept that gift is to follow him redemptively.

Let us not dogmatize over the precise method and technique of entering a redemptive relationship with Christ. To some people it does happen dramatically, as it did to Paul on the Damascus Road—one great climactic experience overshadowing all the rest of life. For others it may consist in a multitude of small daily decisions, a gradual reorientation of life, an intensification of those finer Christian values implanted within our personality from childhood. There was nothing supernatural about John Wesley's conversion. He did not become ecstatic, or burst into tears, or leap in the air. Few people realized what had happened to him. He simply felt strangely warmed within, like any person does when he stumbles upon a new truth. In an ordinary service of worship there came to Wesley the honest conviction, which had probably been forming in his mind for years, that Christ was his Saviour: "I felt that he had taken away my sins, even mine, and saved me from the law of sin and death. . . ." Wesley had always believed in Christ, had been a minister of Christ, but now, for the first time in a conscious act of decision, a deliberate venture of faith, he committed his life to Christ. A man really becomes a Christian when he does that.

III

A Christian is a man who responds to the Master's call "Follow me!", and another part of his response will be a *devotional* relationship to Christ. The life of devotion provides us with our means of extending that brief period of earthly fellowship between the historic Jesus and his disciples. This has been the most thrilling discovery of believers through the ages—that he whom they follow is no dead, historical figure, but a living Presence who could be to them everything he was to the Galilean fishermen just so long as they opened their lives to the means of his continuing influence.

Christ himself has provided those means; we call them "the means of grace". Such is the Bible, and especially those books known as Gospels. We have all had the experience of reading a biography so skilfully written that its subject walked right out of the pages and became one of our personal friends. The Gospels are all of that to us. We read them and we come into living fellowship with the Incarnate Son of God. We listen to him teaching the multitudes and we catch the unmistakable note of Divine authority. We feel the tenderness of his touch on the wasted limbs of lepers and the firmness of his grasp on the trembling shoulders of a demoniac. We weep with him over the city that was to reject him and we mourn at the sight of his tortured agony on the Cross. The Gospels are all of that and more, because the soul has eyes to perceive a Reality behind the written words of Scripture. As we read in the power of the Holy Spirit, the centuries slip away, the Gospel story becomes our story, and Christ is present with us here and now.

Our Lord taught us to pray, and he uses our prayers as a means of bringing his gracious influence to bear upon our lives. Perhaps we cannot help envying the disciples their face to face companionship with the historic Jesus. What a privilege to have been singled out from all generations in history to walk this common earth in comradeship with the great Revealer of God! But the Christian life is always an adventure in comradeship with Christ, and though we cannot see him, yet we know that he walks beside us and that in prayer we have a means of quickening the sense of his presence. Prayer in its highest form is holy conversation with Christ, and the serious Christian will guard it jealously and diligently. He will keep inviolate that daily period of devotion when he withdraws from the world and enters the secret place there to commune consciously with his living Lord.

In our distinctive act of Christian worship, the Sacrament of his body and blood, Christ has provided a channel of Divine grace into our lives. At his own Table he communes with us. There we partake of bread and wine, visible signs of his real Presence in our midst; there we see dramatized a story old but ever new, the living and dying of the Lord Jesus, the Word made flesh, dwelling among us, full of grace and truth. This happens in all true worship, for the same Christ who confronts us in the broken bread, confronts us in the spoken Word. How utterly mistaken the claim that a man can be a Christian without attending public worship! How can any man presume to follow Christ unless he avails himself of those means of devotion which Christ himself has provided?

IV

The Christian life has also an *institutional* relationship to Christ. This is another way of saying that the man who tries to follow Christ will try to be the best possible member of Christ's Church. He will not be impatient with the Church's weakness and stodginess—unavoidable because the Church is a mixed company—but he will remember that the Church is Christ's own creation and not just an optional religious society that came into being because a group of like-minded people decided that there should be one. When Jesus said to the disciples, "Follow me!", he called them into a fellowship; and when he passed from human sight he left behind him a fellowship, promising that within that fellowship we should meet him and grow in the knowledge of him and continue his earthly ministry as in no other way.

How vividly the New Testament describes this organic oneness between Christ and his Church and between Christian believers themselves. It sees the Church related to Christ as a flock to its shepherd; as branches finding their source of life in a single Vine; as a building, a massive structure rising through the ages, its joints and arches all interrelated and resting upon the one foundation of Christ. It sees the Church as Christ's body, that new human organism which he chose as the tabernacle of his living Presence and in which the members have a vital unity like the arms, muscles, bones and arteries of a human body. These New Testament metaphors all add up to the same truth—that Christ and his Church are one and indivisible, that a relationship to the one implies a relationship to the other, and that only in fellowship with other Christians can we find a true fellowship with Christ.

An old and beautiful legend relates that Zacchaeus, after he had been converted, used to rise early every morning and leave the house. His wife was curious to know where he went and what he did, so one morning she followed him. At the town well he lowered a bucket, filled it with water, went out through the city gates and walked until he came to a sycamore tree. There, setting down the bucket of water, he began to gather and cast away the stones and branches and rubbish that lay about the foot of the tree. Having done this he poured water on the roots of the tree and, gently caressing the trunk with his hands, stood silent as if in affectionate reminiscence and contemplation. When his amazed wife came out of her hiding-place and asked what he was doing, Zacchaeus replied, "This is where I found Christ." For nineteen centuries, people have borne that same tender, affectionate witness concerning the Church, "This is where I found Christ."

There is no meaning to the hackneyed question, "Can a man be a Christian outside the Church?" As well ask, "Can a nose be a nose without a face?" Preachers often recall the incident of that man who said to his minister, "I don't need to go to church to be a Christian"; and the minister replied by taking a live coal from the open fireplace and laying it alone on the hearth where it turned grey and black and cold and dead. Then he restored it to the fire among the other coals where it soon came to life and burned brightly again. The real question is not whether a Christian needs the Church's fellowship, but whether he can be a vital Christian without labouring devotedly for the Church's witness and mission. The man who really tries to follow Christ will know that whatever has been accomplished in the name of Christ through nineteen centuries has been accomplished not by single piccolos and flutes tooting their little isolated tunes, but by the great symphony of the Church playing harmoniously under its Divine Conductor; and he will ask no higher privilege than to be a member of that symphony and to play his part, however obscure, in making the Church strong and effectual.

v

The the Christian life has its *ethical* relationship to Christ. Of course, it were a form of idolatry to make this single point of the star the sum total of our discipleship and to construct, as many people do construct, a religion based entirely on Christian moral principles. Ethics are the fruit, not the root of Christian experience, but the tree must bear fruit else Christ himself will curse and condemn it.

The truth is that a man ought never to be the same again once he has responded to the Master's call and declared himself to be a follower of Christ; and if we Christians ignore that truth, then the world will quickly force it upon our attention. We can feel complimented that those outside the Church sometimes accuse us of hypocrisy, for it indicates that they do expect us to be governed by a higher standard of morals than they normally apply to themselves. They know that though one must be tough to get ahead in business, yet a man who passes the offering plate on Sunday will on Monday temper his toughness with integrity and charity. Though homes break asunder every day through impatience and infidelity, yet a Christian home will be a centre of forbearance and sacrificial love. Though he lives in a day of relaxed moral standards when voices from every direction shout in his ear urging him to live like an animal, yet the follower of Christ, because he is a follower of Christ, will accept voluntarily the discipline of Christian manhood. Though society abounds in frivolous, luxury-loving people, who care for no one but themselves, yet the Christian will have about him a serious and unselfish concern. We may have some difficulty in deciding upon the exact theological definition of a Christian, but we still know that in every circumstance there is a Christian thing to do, a Christian word to speak, a Christian way to react and a Christian decision to make.

A Christian is a man who tries to be a follower of Jesus Christ. When you follow a leader in any area of life, you bind yourself to imitate him. If, for example, as a violinist you are a follower of Jascha Heifitz, it means that you hold up Heifitz as your ideal, you copy his techniques, his interpretations; you make him your master. Jesus is the master of life. He came to earth not only to show us God, but to show us human life lived at its highest and best. You remember Peter's amazing reaction to that miracle on the seashore when Jesus ordered him to cast his net overboard and he drew it in full of fishes. Peter said, "Depart from me, for I am a sinful man, O Lord!" Astonishing! Why should Peter suddenly want to push Jesus away from him? Why? Because he recognized that before him stood one who embodied the power, the grace, the holiness and the moral perfection of God, and Peter, always a realist, knew how difficult it would be to live with that power and grace and holiness and perfection. "Depart from me! . . . How can you, being what you are, and I, being what I am, inhabit the same order of reality?" The answer is that, being what we are, we cannot. To live with Christ we must be different; we must share the life of

Christ, his character, his values, his motives, his ideals. To follow Christ we must try to be Christlike.

One day the philosopher, Josiah Royce, was sitting in his study at Harvard University talking with a young student. In the course of the conversation the student asked the professor, "What is your definition of a Christian?" The great philosopher replied, "I do not know how to define a Christian. . . . But wait," he added, looking out of the window, "there goes Phillips Brooks." That was his definition, a walking definition, for of Phillips Brooks it could be said that he lived a life perfectly related to Jesus Christ. Once when a young man wrote to him asking him to share the secret of his life, he replied, "It is a deeper knowledge and a truer love of Christ. . . . I cannot tell you how personal this grows to me. He is here. He knows me and I know him." One of the finest monuments in America stands outside Trinity Church, Boston, and it depicts this saintly man in his pulpit. Christ stands beside him, his hand resting on the preacher's shoulder. Of the sculptor it is said that he came to see that Phillips Brooks could not be explained apart from Jesus Christ. And there, perhaps, is our only valid definition, our only convincing answer to the question with which we began. By no preachment can we really satisfy that earnest inquirer who asked, "What is a Christian?" But I wonder if we could point him to someone we know, someone who has responded to the Master's call and who so tries to follow Jesus that of him it might be said, "*There* goes a Christian."

2

MAKING AN IDOL OF RELIGION

"Jesus said, 'I tell you, something greater than the temple is
here.' "

(St. Matthew 12:6)

NELS FERRÉ has written a searching little book entitled *The Sun and the Umbrella*.[1] He begins with a
parable, obviously drawn from his own imagination,
about a race of people who called themselves Sun-worshippers. Once they had been part of a much larger company
living in a badly lighted old barn known as the House of
Legality. A young prophet came to them one day and told
them that there was bright sunshine outside. That angered
some of them and they put him to death. Others believed
him, however, and went out to live in the sun. For some
reason, though, they seemed unable to endure the direct
sunlight, so they put up an umbrella upon which they wrote,
"We are the Sun-worshippers." Then certain wise men
collected writings about the prophet, and erected a small
umbrella under the first large one. Disputes arose about the
interpretation of these writings, whereupon other men constructed a third umbrella inside the second; they called it
The Church and on it wrote, "We are the true Sun-worshippers. Outside this umbrella no one can be sure of the sun."
After that, many smaller umbrellas sprang up over creeds
and dogmas and liturgies and forms of ecclesiastical government, each sheltering groups who, though they called themselves Sun-worshippers, refused to come out and live under
the direct light of the sun.

[1] Nels F. Ferré (Harper and Brothers, New York 1953)

It is possible to worship religion instead of worshipping God. We hear a great deal about idolatry these days, the gods that modern men worship; the gods of money, power, pleasure and skill. Idolatry has a long history, going back to Old Testament times, but its essential nature remains unchanged: men worship the creature instead of the creator; they give to the work of their own hands the loyalty and obedience due only unto him who made and sustains all things; they pin their ultimate faith on values which are derivative and secondary. Do we realize that the most subtle of all idolatries is religion? That very structure of belief and practice through which we relate ourselves to God may cease to be a means of grace and may become an end in itself, an idol to be worshipped and adored. The avenue of approach to God may become more important to us than God himself, and the temple of God's presence more sacred than the presence which it enshrines.

"Jesus said, 'I tell you something greater than the temple is here.'" But pious Jews recognized nothing greater than the temple, nothing holier than their most holy religion. They were religious people, but they were not godly people. In fact, they were so religious that they had lost sight of God, otherwise they might have recognized the presence of God in this man whom they crucified as a blasphemer. There are at least four elements in our relationship with God, four umbrellas, all of them integral to high and vital religion, yet all of which people tend to idolize and to worship in place of God himself.

I

First, the *Bible*. The Bible is central in Protestant Christianity. Truly we are the people of a Book. We acknowledge the Bible as our supreme authority, higher than any human voice or ecclesiastical pronouncement, that objective authority beyond the Church's life through which God speaks to the Church, judges the Church and corrects its whole existence. We believe that the Old and New Testament Scriptures are so organically related to the event of God's act of salvation in Christ as to be a constitutive part of that event. That same eternal Word of God which once became flesh in Jesus of Nazareth confronts us now in the written words that bear witness to him. Through the Bible we relate ourselves to Christ as in no other way. The Bible is an indispensable means of grace.

To confuse means with ends, however, and to make the printed page of this very human collection of books an end in itself were to be guilty of what we call Bibliolatry. We mean by Bibliolatry the reduction of the Bible to the level of a text-book on religion, of the same order as a text-book on history or mathematics. In such a view the Bible becomes a magic document, each chapter, each word, each punctuation mark dictated inerrantly by God and dictated in a seventeenth-century translation. In this view the King James Version of the Bible becomes infallible, a paper pope, as contrasted to the living Pope in Rome. Those who hold it believe that the Bible as God's Word is not only definitive, but terminal. Whatever God intends to say to the human race he has already said. "It's in the Book," there for everyone to read—a view which, carried to its logical extreme, makes God himself no longer necessary.

Professor Ferré suggests that people who worship the Scriptures would obviously rather have God as a pen-pal than as a personal companion—which is hardly a mature and satisfactory relationship. A man may have received numerous love letters from his wife before their marriage, yet if their relationship is right and real, he does not need to examine continually his present understanding of her in the light of her past utterances. On a quiet Sunday afternoon he may refresh and rekindle his memory by reading some of her old letters, but she herself is still the centre of his attention and affection. True love lives in the present. So the Bible, while a record of God's mighty acts in history and therefore a constant means of grace, is no substitute for our knowledge and love of God in the living Spirit.

Someone has drawn this analogy. Consider a window-pane which, if you look at it directly, serves no useful purpose. You have to look through the window-pane and focus your attention on what lies beyond. Thus the Christian looks not at the Bible itself, but through the Bible to the encounters between God and man which are described on the printed page. If we allow our vision to stop with the printed page itself, its statements and propositions, the image beyond may be blurred, and we shall not come to know God as fully as we should. But if we read the Bible and at the same time look through the Bible, then it serves as a kind of window by means of which God and Christ and man and sin and salvation are brought into true focus. The Bible remains our highest authority, but we shall not forget that something greater than the Bible is here.

II

We tend also to idolize *theology*. By theology we mean that structure of religious faith which men have formulated in creeds through the centuries. Certainly there can be no such thing as a creedless religion. Every man lives by some fixed body of belief, whether it be a belief in dialectical materialism or in the revelation of love as the controlling principle of this universe. Creeds are to religion what maps are to geography. The early explorers who landed on the shores of North America drew maps of the regions through which they travelled. They realized that beyond these charted areas lay an entire continent as yet unknown to them, but they drew maps of what they did know for the guidance of future generations. So through the centuries men have experienced something of God, only the fringe of his infinite, mysterious Being, but something none the less, and of what they have experienced they have formulated creeds, religious maps for the guidance of future generations.

Studying maps, however fascinating an occupation, is no substitute for visiting a country itself. Yet men have done exactly that with their creeds. They have given the knowledge of God a greater glory than they have given to God himself. W. A. Gifford, my old Church History Professor, repeatedly spoke about what he called "the Catholic Mind"— the dogmatic, imperialistic, totalitarian mind which emerged in the Christianity of the Middle Ages, a mind on which Rome had no monopoly. Rudely and arrogantly that mind asserts, "We have the truth, the whole truth! You believe as we do, or you are damned, you're going to hell, you're not a Christian!" Some of the most spectacular bonfires in history have been fed by the bodies of heretics, men who committed the supreme sin of contradicting the catholic mind and renouncing a creed which in the light of their direct experience of God no longer appeared valid.

Credal idolatry is a major stumbling-block in the path of the ecumenical movement. It seems miraculous, this coming together in our day of ecclesiastical bodies which hitherto have regarded one another indifferently and suspiciously, but we should realize that many come to the ecumenical movement with strong reservations. They are willing to converse with other Communions and have fellowship with them, but not on equal terms, for they believe that just as a man in monogamous society can have only one wife, so Christ, according to the New Testament, can have only one Bride, and they have long since appropriated that status for themselves. When the Central Committee of the World Council of Churches met at Toronto in 1950, it issued an extremely precise and carefully balanced statement to the effect that membership in the World Council did not imply that a member Church was obliged to treat the other member Churches as being in the full sense Churches. Each Church recognized that the Church Universal exists in some sense beyond its own boundaries, but the question "in what sense?" must be "a question for common study and discussion".

In his satire, *The Great Divorce*,[1] C. S. Lewis takes us with a busload of ghosts who have made a journey from hell to heaven with a view to remaining there permanently. The party includes a ghost who happens to be wearing gaiters and is obviously a bishop. On earth he had prided himself on his doctrinal integrity, being a thinker of the more liberal school. In heaven he greets a former colleague who had differed from him theologically and at once he resumes the old arguments.

[1] Geoffrey Bles (London 1945)

The "solid person", as Lewis calls the citizen of heaven, invites his ghostly Lordship to stay, but the Bishop declines and says that he must return to hell for an important meeting. "We have a little Theological Society down there," he explains—a new kind of bonfire. The solid person, however, is not interested in discussing theology. He says, "In heaven we know nothing about religion; we think only of Christ." Something greater than theology is here.

III

Another aspect of religion which we tend to idolize is *worship*. I do not believe that there can be any true religion without worship. On our side, worship is the first duty which we owe to God, the fulfilment of our human greatness, the activity which marks us off from the lower creatures. On God's side, worship is a means of grace, an effective channel whereby he communicates himself to us that we may grow in the knowledge of his love and the understanding of his will. The late William Temple believed in worship as the one means by which the world can save itself from political chaos and collapse. He said that to worship is "to quicken the conscience by the holiness of God, to feed the mind with the truth of God, to purge the imagination by the beauty of God, to open up the heart to the love of God, to devote the will to the purpose of God". Worship described in this way includes the whole of life in all its relationships; it cannot be confined to stated occasions; and yet, unless worship does take place on stated occasions it will not take place at all. You hear it said that a man can be a Christian without going to church, but I doubt whether a man can remain radiantly Christian divorced from the fellowship of praise, any more than a coal can remain aflame divorced from the living fire.

At the other extreme we can become so enamoured of worship, so meticulous and fussy about its outward forms, its liturgical correctness and aesthetic appeal, that it ceases to be a means of grace and becomes an end in itself, an idol which stands between the congregation and God. Every minister fights the temptation to compose prayers and preach sermons which by their sheer brilliance and originality distract the worshippers from God, just as a gaudy frame distracts our attention from a masterpiece of art. We forget that the greatest of all preachers after Christ described himself as an earthen vessel, "that the excellency of the power may be of God and not of us". On one occasion when our service was being televised, I heard the producer refer to it as the "show". He said, "We have to keep this show within sixty minutes." Noticing me, he apologized for this slip of his tongue, but I reassured him that many people do regard Sunday worship as a nervously clocked hour of religious entertainment, and the show had better be good or they won't be back next week.

Most ministers possess a rather bulky file of anonymous letters, and many of them concern the trivia of public worship, little things like hymn tunes and choir gowns and formal prayers, that are not going to make any real difference to the Kingdom of God. A visitor, who had worshipped in one of my churches, subsequently addressed an unsigned letter in which he deplored the "hideous architecture" of the sanctuary and referred to ours as "the most poorly conducted Communion Service" which he had ever attended. He suggested that my sermon was "too strident and forceful for a thoughtful Communion meditation", castigated the "feeble choir support" and rebuked me for wearing an academic hood to the Lord's Table. From his reference one got the impression that he travels widely and visits many churches. In fact, he styles himself as an authority on churches, a connoisseur of preaching and an expert on public worship. I could not help wondering whether he derives any good from public worship, whether it does anything for his soul and brings him into communion with God.

There is a penetrating dialogue on the subject of worship in the New Testament. It took place between Jesus and a woman who boasted a rather colourful record of legalized adultery (five marriages and now a common-law relationship). When Jesus touched this exposed nerve in the woman's soul, she tried the familiar expedient of redirecting the conversation along impersonal lines. "I see you are a prophet," she said, "so let's have a discussion about religion. We Samaritans worship on this mountain, but you Jews believe that Jerusalem is the place where men ought to worship." And what answer did Jesus give? He said, "Look, this business of where and how men ought to worship has its place in religion, but a place of secondary importance. What really matters when you worship is that you stand in absolute honesty before God. And the time for that is now, because something greater than worship is here."

IV

Then there are Christians who idolize the *Church*, giving to the Church a greater devotion than they give to the Church's Lord. In their zeal they come closer to reality than do spiritual isolationists who hold themselves aloof from the historic Christian fellowship, despising the Church as a mere human convenience which one may join or leave alone. There is no question that Christ established the Church as the place of his living Presence. Someone has said, "Having taken humanity upon himself, Christ has not again divested himself of it. As Son of Man he is at the right hand of the Father, and his Spirit is given to the Church which is his body on earth." To the question, "Can a man be a Christian apart from the Church?" the New Testament replies, "Can a leg or an arm have any usefulness or even remain alive apart from the human body to which it belongs?"

Yet it were equally wrong to worship the human institution and so to idolize the Church and become so wrapped up in the service of the Church that we forget the Lord of whom the Church is but an instrument. Pierre Boulle's successfully filmed novel, *The Bridge on the River Kwai*, contains a parable of deep religious significance. A battalion of British soldiers, detained in a Japanese prison camp, is compelled to construct a bridge that will facilitate the movement of enemy troops. For the sake of morale their colonel insists that the men work efficiently and build a bridge of which they can be proud. He himself becomes so obsessed with this material structure that he loses sight of the whole purpose of the war, he forgets whose side he is fighting on, and when a higher British command moves in to dynamite the bridge, it is he who nearly frustrates the scheme.

As the bridge became to the British colonel, so the Church becomes to many Christians, an idol to be worshipped and preserved at all costs, a mere structure that takes on greater importance than the overall campaign of God and becomes in the end a hindrance to the Kingdom. Often I lie awake at night wondering about the purpose of my ministry— whether I labour unceasingly to work the works of God, or simply to build up a human institution called the City Temple, keep it strong, vigorous, successful and important. Sometimes I come away from a church conference wondering if the Cross has not been supplanted by a denominational Year Book, a proud statistical record of numerical strength, financial assets, and vested interest to which we cling with a jealous devotion. The question haunts me—What is God doing in the world? What purpose does he have for his Church? Can it be that he intends eventually to blow it up?

We can be sure of this: God does not intend his visible Church to survive indefinitely, for though Christ left a Church behind him, and though it is indispensable to his continuing ministry, yet Christ did not come to establish a Church but to establish a Kingdom. The Church itself is not that Kingdom. The Church points to the Kingdom, preaches the Kingdom and works for the Kingdom, but it will lose its life in order that the Kingdom may be finally accomplished. The Church lives only to die, to labour and to suffer in this "time between the times", until its existence as an institution becomes no longer necessary, because men everywhere shall accept Christ as Saviour and worship him as Lord.

In the closing chapters of the Book of Revelation we see a glorious vision of the end of all history. Earth's warfare has ended, the legions of death have been vanquished, Satan crushed absolutely and God's righteous age has begun. From heaven descends the New Jerusalem, "prepared as a bride adorned for her husband". "And I saw no temple there," says the writer, "for its temple is the Lord God the Almighty and the Lamb." The Holy City has no need of a Church, because the city is itself the Church, the ingathering of all tribes and nations into one great people of God, their life forever illuminated by the light of Christ and eternally cleansed from all sorrow and evil.

During the war a navy chaplain preached a power-packed sermon on the Ten Commandments. One sailor left the service very much depressed by a consciousness of having done evil in the sight of the Lord all up and down the line. He brightened, however, and said to himself, "Well, at least I've never worshipped a graven image." He was probably wrong. For what is a graven image in modern terms? Anything that man himself has created, be it a house in the suburbs or a bank account or a political system or even the human elements in his religion. We worship idols whenever we look to something creaturely as a basis of faith, as if it were a more certain basis than God himself. Let us heed this warning of Richard Baxter, "Above all the plagues on this side of hell, see that you watch and pray against settling anywhere short of heaven, or reposing your souls on anything below God." "Jesus said, 'I tell you, something greater than the temple is here.'"

3

ALL THE FULNESS OF CHRIST

IT SEEMS a human failing in any area of thought and experience to fasten on part of the truth and espouse it as the whole truth. Like most ministers I receive occasional letters, some signed, some anonymous, which have as their burden the "fulness" of the Gospel. Someone will write saying, "Dear Mr. Griffith: I attended worship in your church last Sunday, and I thank you for your sermon. It is good these days to hear a man who preaches the 'full Gospel'. . . ." Or someone will write less charitably, "Dear Sir: If your sermons are typical of the modern pulpit, then I don't see much hope for the Church. Why cannot you ministers preach the 'full Gospel'?" Rarely do these correspondents, generous or critical, go on to explain what they mean by that ambiguous phrase "full Gospel", but I think it not unkind to say that they usually imply that particular part of Christian truth which appeals to their understanding, which has helped them, and which they have now exalted to the status of whole truth.

In North America there seem to be three such emphases in the thought and experience of Christian people. Each is valid, and yet each has been dogmatized to a point where it tacitly denies the validity of the other two. Each has been made into a cult with its own high priest, its own apostles, its own interpretation of the Scriptures, its own theology, and sometimes its own Church.

There is the "crisis" cult which until recently was kept alive by those off-brand perimeter sects whose people worship in Gospel Halls and sing jazzy hymns and boast of believing in the "plenary interpretation of the Scriptures" and whisper in each other's ear, "Are you saved, my brother?"

However, there seems to be a renaissance of religious funda-
mentalism in some of the established North American
churches, even the more decorous ones. Certain theological
schools have split over the issue, and local congregations find
it necessary to screen a minister's theology before calling him.
Billy Graham is the high priest of this neo-fundamentalism.
We must not write him off as a mere Bible-belt evangelist,
putting on bigger and better revival meetings of a type that
many of us staid Protestants react against. He is more than
a literal-minded, narrow interpreter of Scripture who ignores
the Biblical scholarship of the past hundred years. Billy
Graham is a gifted and dedicated servant of God who proclaims a prophetic word urgently needed by our generation.
A modern John the Baptist, he sounds forth the forgotten
note of God's judgment and warns us to flee from the wrath
to come. So far as he is concerned, the world's salvation
begins with you and me, with a crisis in our souls—the ad-
mission of sin and the repentance which humbly seeks forgiveness.

Then there is the "Peace of Mind" cult which borrows
heavily from the teachings of Christian Science and which in
North America has been so fascinatingly commended by its
urbane high priest, Norman Vincent Peale. Peale claims to
preach the full Gospel. Recently he told a newspaper, "Over
the years what I have tried to do in my simple way is to
preach the Gospel, the old, Christ-centred, Church-centred,
Holy Spirit-centred Gospel." Peale's most popular book is
entitled *The Power of Positive Thinking*. Judging from its
phenomenal sales, this book surely offers men and women in
this tense, complicated, fear-stricken, mid-twentieth century
the gospel which they feel they most desperately need.
Crammed with "confidence-concepts", "faith-attitudes",
"energy-producing thoughts" and "spirit-lifters", it con-
strues religion as a sure-fire means of getting what you want
out of life. It presents God as a vast reservoir of obedient
power which we can manipulate for our own purposes, just
as we can manipulate steam and electricity and atomic
energy for our own purposes, a power which we may control
more and more effectively as we learn the proper technique.

To multitudes of distraught people this is exactly what they have been waiting for; all previous religious insights they discard on a rubbish heap. The moment they read Peale, they feel like Archimedes who leaped out of a bathtub and ran down the streets, naked, shouting, "I have found it." As one man said to me, reverently fondling a copy of Peale's book, "To this I owe my salvation!" and I didn't doubt him.

There is a third cult in North American Christianity. We shall call it the cult of activism. It is more a cult of the muscles than of the conscience or mind. If it speaks at all, it says something like this, "Don't bother me with morbid theories of sin and salvation; don't talk to me about the power of positive thinking. Just give me something Christian to *do*. Let me work my way to heaven!" He might recoil at the very thought of it, but I think we must designate Elton Trueblood as the modern high priest of religious activism. Trueblood is the great proponent of lay religion. In his numerous books he keeps coming back to his pet theory—the disadvantages of being an ordained minister and the advantages of being a layman. With his Quaker background he has an impatience with theology and a natural dislike for formal and ordered worship. He considers that worship achieves its true value as a kind of religious pep-talk, a briefing session for practical Christians in their task of witnessing. Trueblood has just the right word for a great many Marthas in the Church who would throw theology out of the window, make worship short and snappy, and roll up their sleeves and get on with the business of serving Christ in a practical way.

Such are the three major emphases in North American Christianity. Each has a legitimate place in the mind and ministry of Jesus and therefore in the total Gospel of salvation. To illustrate this, let us consider a single New Testament episode. On one occasion when Jesus and the disciples had crossed the Sea of Galilee to the country of the Gerasenes, they were met by an insane man who emerged from his dwelling-place among the tombs of the dead. Seeing Jesus, this demoniac let out an unearthly scream, "What have you to do with me, Jesus, Son of the Most High God? I beseech you, do not torment me!" With courage and compassion

Jesus healed the man; he sent the spirits that possessed him into a nearby herd of swine, and the pigs rushed headlong over a cliff into the sea. Jesus *had* to do this in order to convince the man, who believed in demons, that he was healed. The news spread quickly, and at once people came out from the city to see this man whom they had given up as dead, now sitting at the feet of Jesus, clothed, and in his right mind. However, they considered a herd of pigs too high a price to pay for a man's sanity; and the poor fellow, if only to escape the anger of his fellow-citizens, begged Jesus to take him away. But Jesus refused. "Return to your home," he said, "and declare how much God has done for you."

Expounding this brief but highly dramatic story, the late David Roberts finds in it three different pictures of Jesus.[1] First, as a *Tormentor*. "What have you to do with me, Jesus, Son of the Most High God? I beseech you, do not torment me!" If you want to miss the whole point of that story, then write off this outcry as the ravings of a demented man with whom you have nothing in common. The truth is that people have always resisted the presence of Jesus. He still torments them, still churns up a crisis in their souls.

Alcibiades said of Socrates, "There is one experience I have in the presence of this man alone, such as nobody would expect in me; and that is, to be made to feel ashamed; he alone can make me feel it. For he brings home to me that I cannot disown the duty of doing what he bids me, but that as soon as I turn from his company I fall a victim to the favours of a crowd." Jesus of Nazareth had that effect on men. He disturbed them, he tormented them, he set going a crisis in their souls. They had felt quite satisfied with themselves until he came along; now they could not live beside him and still be what they were.

Do you remember how Ivan, the most intellectual member of that weird trio, The Brothers Karamazov, tells of the poem which he has written called *The Grand Inquisitor*? The scene is set in Seville the day after the burning of heretics in one of those bloody carnivals which made the sixteenth century so

[1] David E. Roberts, *The Grandeur and Misery of Man* (Oxford University Press, New York 1955), p. 22ff.

lurid. Christ had come to visit his people. The tortured folk
flocked to him. He healed the blind. A little seven-year-old
girl was borne in her white coffin down the steps of the cathedral. Softly he whispered to her, "*Talitha cumi*," and answering, she arose and looked wonderingly about. With a frown
the Grand Inquisitor stood watching. Suddenly and sternly
he pointed to Jesus and snapped out an order, "Arrest that
man!" Hours later he stole into the dungeon with his lantern.
There he upbraided the prisoner bitterly for coming to earth
again and upsetting what little human authority the Church
had managed to contrive. His eyes seemed to burn through
the darkness with fanatic fire. On and on he poured the
tumult of his speech until it spent itself in the threat and
sentence of death. Christ never said a word. Quietly, in the
silence that fell, he drew near and kissed the old man on his
bloodless lips. That was the whole answer. And those lips
began to tremble. The eyes that burned with fire slowly
widened. The Grand Inquisitor stumbled blindly to the door.
He threw it open and screamed, "Go, and come no more!
Come not at all, never, never!"

Jesus Christ remains the most tormenting influence in the
world today. Life would be infinitely more placid for all of us
if the New Testament and the story of Christianity and the
Church and the presence of Christian people and the living
Christ could be blotted from our experience as the Communists expurgate their history books. Peace of mind? A man
has that after a good dinner when his pipe is drawing well.
He does not have it when he opens the Bible and allows the
hurricane of incarnate holiness to disturb the green scum
which has settled on the stagnant pool of his soul. For years
I have tried to figure out why some people never darken the
door of a church, and I know the reason: they do not want
to be disturbed; they do not want a tormenting presence
trespassing on the private reserves of their own self-
satisfaction. Writes T. S. Eliot:

"Why should men love the Church? Why should they love
  her laws?
She tells them of Life and Death, and of all they would
  forget.

She is tender where they would be hard, and hard where
                        they like to be soft,
She tells them of Evil and Sin, and other unpleasant facts.''[1]

Christ the Tormentor! Apart from him I can lead a smug, selfish, unexamined life; but let me enter his presence, let me catch a vision of him dying upon the Cross, and I know that something is wrong between me and God, radically, emphatically and decisively wrong, and that only he in his mercy and grace can put it right.

The second picture shows Christ as a *Healer*. We find the demoniac sitting there, clothed, and in his right mind. Many of our Lord's contemporaries, especially the Pharisees, could not be rid of him quickly enough, because he tormented them; but that was not the purpose of his ministry. "I am come," he said, "that they might have life and have it abundantly." And such life he proffered to people, full life, joyous, abundant, eternal life charged with meaning and purpose. Jesus rescued men and women from a living death. He gave soundness to their broken bodies and sanity to their distraught minds; he restored the integrity of their personalities and made them whole again. The same holiness which stirs up a crisis in the souls of men brings with it the greatest healing power that the world has ever known.

Christianity is only half a Gospel, and therefore no Gospel at all, unless its conflicts issue in restoration and wholeness. It is said that Robert Burns might have been a different man if the Scottish divines of his day had preached a Gospel that heals as well as torments. They thundered the law and the judgment, but stopped there, and their condemnation threw Burns back on his own resources. Like the Prodigal Son he often repented and said, "I will go home to my Father," but he never saw the Father as Jesus revealed him, the Friend of every defeated soul who came to seek and to save the lost. Christ *does* give peace of mind. He gives the peace of reconciliation with God and therefore the faith that we are not alone in an uncaring universe but are in the hands of a Divine goodness and mercy and power; the faith that God is

[1] T. S. Eliot, Chorus VI from *The Rock*, Faber and Faber Ltd., London, 1934; Harcourt, Brace and World, Inc., New York, 1936.

with us and that with him there is forgiveness for sin, solace for sorrow, strength and courage for living in all situations.

Norman Cousins begins his recent word picture of Albert Schweitzer by describing the regular after-dinner ritual in the jungle hospital at Lambaréné.[1] The great doctor announced the hymn to be sung and walked over to an upright piano on the other side of the room where he sat down to play. The piano, says Cousins, must have been at least fifty years old. The keyboard was badly stained. Large double screws fastened the ivory to each note. One or more strings were missing on at least a dozen keys. Under equatorial conditions of extreme heat and moisture you do not even try to keep a piano in tune. And now, one of the world's great musicians, the greatest living interpreter of Bach's organ music, sat down to play this dilapidated old instrument. The amazing and wondrous thing, writes Norman Cousins, was that the piano seemed to lose its poverty in his hands. Its tinniness and clattering echoes seemed subdued. Its capacity to yield music was now being fully realized. Whatever the reason, Schweitzer's presence at the piano seemed to make it right.

Christ performs that miracle with a human personality. He, the Master of Life, takes a human character, however broken and dilapidated, and as long as it is entirely sensitive to his touch, he brings out the best in it. More amazing and wondrous still, Christ heals human personality; he not only brings harmony out of disharmony, but he repairs the damaged instrument, restores its strength, its resilience, its capacity to yield noble and joyous music.

The third picture shows Christ as *Master*. The restored man wanted to remain close to Jesus and become one of the disciples, but Jesus sent him home to tell his own townsfolk the news of his salvation; and that was a difficult assignment, because already he had gotten himself blacklisted for his share in the destruction of the pigs. But then, Jesus was always handing out difficult assignments. He told his followers that they had to be more righteous than the

[1] Norman Cousins, *Dr. Schweitzer of Lambaréné* (Harper and Brothers, Publishers, New York 1960), pp. 9 and 10.

Scribes and Pharisees, that they must be prepared to love their enemies to forgive an unlimited number of times and to persevere in well-doing even when people kicked them in the face for it. After his resurrection he gave these ordinary men the breathtaking responsibility for the extension of his Kingdom throughout the world. It was all a matter of simple logic: he, the Master, had walked the way of sacrificial love; therefore those who followed him must walk the way of sacrificial love.

How can we fail to see this picture of Jesus? I find it astonishing that any person who has attended church for many years and exposed himself to the Christ of the Gospels, should still be able to lead an ingrown and self-indulgent life. When you read the biographies of great Christians, you invariably come to that decisive experience where a man really surrenders his life to Jesus Christ, and from that moment onward he lives no longer for himself but for Christ who loved him and died for him. Instead of seeking to create a comfortable nest for himself on earth, he seeks first the Kingdom of God and his righteousness. He has only one question now: "Lord, what wilt thou have me to do?" He lives on the principle that whoever would save his life must lose it, and he does lose it; with a reckless abandon he fairly flings away his energy, his gifts, his time, his money—throws them at the feet of Christ, the Master, whose Lordship demands all that we have and all that we are.

What do people do when they profess to believe in the "full Gospel"? At Benson, Arizona, about twenty families of a group known as the Full Gospel Assembly disappeared last July. Local authorities eventually found them in underground bomb shelters. Believing that Russia would shortly destroy one-third of the world by nuclear attack, these religious people spent two months digging in the basements of their homes. Just before they vanished, they bought large quantities of food supplies which they stored in their homes and church. Then they covered all windows and doors and even keyholes with newspapers and tape, presumably to guard against radiation dangers. We cannot laugh at the activities of the Full Gospel Assembly; there is something too realistic about them. We can hold them up as an example of effective civil defence. Not as an example of the full Gospel, however, because true followers of Christ will never entomb themselves in their own security and leave the rest of the world to be blown up. Not retreat, but *involvement*—that is the word; involvement in the world's misery and suffering and fear and chaos and death, the involvement of a Cross.

So we look at the story of the Gerasene Demoniac and we see Christ in all his fulness. These three pictures comprise the "full" Gospel, and to fix upon any one of them to the exclusion of the others is to hold a partial and inadequate Gospel. Some people are obsessed with Christ the Tormentor; their great mission in life is to convince the rest of us that we are miserable sinners. Others talk about the joy and serenity of our religion; in their cheeriness and sentimentality they sometimes ignore the tragedies and sufferings of the world about them. Finally, there are those energetic, practical people for whom religion means such a continuous round of good works and committee meetings that the rest of us become exhausted trying to keep up with them. The point is that each has part of the truth but not the whole truth. We capture the full Gospel only by relating the whole of life to Christ in all his fulness. To let him quicken our consciences, to find in him joy and serenity, to receive from him the imperative to carry forward the practical tasks that lie before us in this troubled world—that is the "full" Gospel wherein we find our salvation.

4

CAN HUMAN NATURE BE CHANGED?

"Nicodemus said to him, 'How can a man be born when he is old?' "

(St. John 3 :4)

I F Y O U were asked in the light of your knowledge of the Bible and your understanding of the ministry of Jesus and your reading of history and your acquaintance with the biographies of great saints and your personal friendship with righteous and godly men, to single out what appeals to you as the essential, the constitutive experience of the Christian life, what would it be? Would it not be that rather old-fashioned and unsophisticated experience which we call "conversion", the turning-about of one's loyalties, the reversal of one's values, and the bisection of one's life into two periods—"before" and "after"? This kind of experience came to the great Russian, Leo Tolstoi. In the middle age of his life he wrote :

> "Five years ago I came to believe in Christ and my life suddenly changed. I ceased to desire what I had previously desired and began to desire what I formerly did not want. What previously seemed to me good seemed evil, and what seemed evil seemed good. It happened to me as it happens to a man who goes out on some business and on the way suddenly decides that the business is unnecessary and returns home. All that was on his right is now on his left, and all that was on his left is now on his right. The former wish, to get as far as possible from home, has changed into a wish to be as near as possible to it. The direction of my life and my desires became different, and good and evil changed places."

Without such an experience of conversion it is doubtful that a man's life can be radiantly and decisively Christian.

41

So Jesus declared to Nicodemus, the educated, urbane and wealthy Pharisee who came under cover of night to discuss religion with him. It indicated our Lord's respect for this man's intelligence that he did not waste time in subtlety and tact, but came to the point with almost crude immediacy and precision. He told Nicodemus, in effect, that no man reasons or works his way into the Kingdom of God. The religious life is not a slow process of cultivation whereby we grow into an understanding of this or that religious dogma and to an acceptance of this or that rule of conduct. The secret of Christian experience lies not in becoming an *improved* person, but in becoming a *changed* person, altogether different from the person you are now. This change Jesus described with a figure of speech. He said to Nicodemus, "Except a man be born again, he cannot see the Kingdom of God" . . . unless, figuratively speaking, he dies and begins life all over again, he will not enter that saving relationship with God that gives him a sense of eternal security.

This strikes an answering chord in our hearts. As a theological concept the conversion experience of second birth may baffle us, and we may care very little for high-flown theories about sin and salvation; but we do care about the worth of our own lives and the lives of our fellows beyond eating, sleeping, working, procreating and dying. However inarticulately, we want something better than we now have, something better than blind fate governing our affairs. We want release from our own weakness and anxiety and self-centredness, release from the mass social forces that sweep us headlong from one catastrophe to another. "Born again!" Where is the man who has not wistfully taken a good look at what he has made of life and thought in terms of what he would change if by some miracle he could go back to the beginning and make a fresh start? Who has not felt dissatisfied with the pattern of living which he has evolved through the years and yearned with Omar Khayyam to smash this sorry scheme of things entire and mould it nearer to his heart's desire? The poet, however, did not believe that his wish could be granted. Cynically he wrote,

" The Moving Finger writes, and having writ
Moves on. Nor all your piety nor wit
Can lure it back to cancel half a line,
Nor all your tears wash out a word of it."

We share the poet's cynicism when the Gospel breaks in upon
us with its radical demands of new life and second birth. We
should like to make a fresh start in life, but that is impossible
because we have lived too long and reached the point of no
return. Our habits, our attitudes, our thought and behaviour
patterns, even our failings and prejudices have become fixed
and congealed. We wish it might be different, but this is what
we have made of life, and now it is too late to change.

That was exactly what bothered Nicodemus. He did not
dispute the Master's claim that the life in God should begin
with a conversion experience of rebirth. He did not deny
that human nature, if it would attain to the image of God,
must be radically and decisively changed. He merely said to
Jesus, "How can a man be born when he is old?" What
stumbled this proud Pharisee was not so much the theory of
the need of new birth as its impracticability. Born again?
How could that be? The man was old; he had lost heart;
his fight seemed over; for him things had become ruthlessly
and inexorably fixed. Once in his youth it might have been
possible, but now he had reached and passed middle age, so
that his chance was gone forever.

I

"How can a man be born when he is old?" There are three
possible ways in which Nicodemus might have asked that
question. First, he might have asked it rhetorically, not as a
question at all, but as a flat denial, perhaps with a tinge of
sarcasm in his voice. "How can a man be born when he is
old?" Can you take a human character which through childhood and adolescence, through training in home and school
and society, through its experience of life and the world has
grown into a certain pattern, and change that pattern as you
would change the paper on a wall? Human nature cannot
be changed! That is a point of view to which many people

subscribe; and they do not regard themselves as cynics but as realists. Indeed, it has become almost axiomatic these days. Let any group come together to discuss the problems of nuclear disarmament, race prejudice or the re-settlement of refugees, and someone is sure to wind up the discussion by saying, "That's all very well, but you can't change human nature." And what we believe about society we believe about ourselves. An old proverb sums up our resignation, "Sow a thought, and you reap an act. Sow an act, and you reap a habit. Sow a habit, and you reap a character. Sow a character, and you reap a destiny."

You cannot change human nature! It is a popular point of view, but it ought not to go unchallenged. At least we should rephrase it in the form of a question and ask with open minds, Can human nature be changed? To be sure, you cannot teach an old dog new tricks, but we are not talking about dogs, intelligent and loveable as they are; we are talking about persons created in the image of God, and it is the belief of a great many students of human nature that persons have been and can be changed. A British preacher of former years expressed the conviction thus: "When you tell me that human nature cannot be changed, I am constrained to reply that in the light of experience, human nature is the only thing that can be changed. We cannot change the laws of the physical world, the ebb and flow of tides, the forces of gravitation and the stars in their courses. But the lives and habits and purposes of men have been and can be changed."

Without reference to religion at all, consider to what extent our modern society is based on the supposition that human nature is capable of being changed. The sciences of the mind, psychology and psychiatry, operate on the premise that you can take a maladjusted human being, made wretched by a collection of repressions and complexes, and by a process of careful analysis change him into a new creature ready to start life all over again with confidence and self-reliance. We spend vast sums of money on the belief that a child of ignorant parents, or an illiterate savage in the jungle, can be taught to read and write, and through a normal process of education be given the key that opens the door to

a new life as different from the old as day is different from
night. Many of our great universities maintain schools of
social work with the express purpose of training men and
women to go out into the world to change people. These
graduates direct boys' clubs, redemptive homes and cor-
rective institutions which take the delinquent, the degenerate
and the criminal, and, despite their heredity and early environment, change them into useful and self-respecting
members of society.

Look at the question negatively. We shall not deny that
human nature can change radically for the worse. Indeed, it
may have been our unhappy experience to meet some person
whom we have not seen for many years and whom we remember for his cheerfulness and outgoing idealism, but who
now appears so callous and sour and cynical and self-
centred that we scarcely recognize him as the same person.
In the Bible the classic example of a personality changed for
the worse is King Saul. The chronicler describes him as a
handsome young man, tall of stature, fair to behold, graced
by his becoming modesty, and admired throughout the land
for his bravery and his qualities of leadership. Is this the same
man whom we see on the throne of Israel, subjected to fits of
brooding melancholy, consumed by his jealousy, flying into
a neurotic rage and crazily flinging his spear at trusted
servants and at his own family? Forgetting the factors which
provoked his radical deterioration in character, we need not
look closely at Saul to reach the conclusion that human
nature can be very definitely and decisively changed.

The Communists believe that human nature can be
changed. David Karp's rather frightening novel, *One*, which
depicts life under a totalitarian régime, tells the story of a
university professor named Burden who, because of a minor
heresy, is imprisoned and subjected to a series of unspeakably
horrible physical and psychological tortures from which he
emerges a totally different personality, a man having no
memory of his past, his family or his profession, a beaten,
timid little man given the new name of Hughes. Has not the
world witnessed this very devilish perversion of the pheno-
menon of rebirth in recent years? Subjected to solitary

45

confinement, to drugs and torture and brainwashing and ceaseless indoctrination, men have emerged from Communist prisons totally different personalities from when they went in, with new loves and hates, new aims and purposes, prepared to renounce their past lives and to sign statements contradicting everything they hitherto believed. Such men have in fact been born again, changed for the worse, it is true, but radically and decisively changed.

How can a man be born when he is old? It is not basically a religious question at all. Our answer comes not from the preachers but from the scientists, even the most cold-blooded scientists of mental phenomena, who tell us that of all living creatures man is the most plastic, and man's nature most subject to change. Argue as we may, it remains a well-authenticated fact that people are reborn, that a human personality may be flowing all in one direction, and then of a sudden seem to reverse itself. Under certain stimuli a human personality can be "formed, deformed and reformed". Human nature *may* not be changed, but it is *capable* of being changed for better or for worse, and therefore we must not rule out as impossible the essential, constitutive experience of the Christian life which Jesus articulated when he said, "Except a man be born again, he cannot see the Kingdom of God."

II

"How can a man be born when he is old?" Let us consider a second possible way in which Nicodemus might have asked this question of Jesus. Perhaps at this point in the conversation this somewhat stuffy Pharisee really warmed up to the discussion and displayed an intelligent and open-minded interest. That is all that Jesus asks of any man. He does not bully us into the Kingdom of God, like the Communist who holds a pistol at your head and says, "Be my brother, or I'll blow your brains out!" The Master of men constrains us into obedience; he constrains us through the winsomeness of his character, the magnetism of his leadership, the sweet reasonableness of his teaching, the appeal of his suffering love

46

upon the Cross and the power of his living Presence in our hearts. Jesus asks only that men be impartial in their attitude to him, that they do not start out on the premise that everything he says must be wrong or insignificant. He asks only that we lay aside our bias and our prejudice and listen to him with open minds, that we weigh his words as intelligently as we weigh the words of any authoritative person and that we give him a fair chance to make something of our lives.

Then let us suppose that Nicodemus reacted in this manner when Jesus told him, "Except a man be born again, he cannot see the Kingdom of God." Let us suppose that he leaned forward and said something like this: "Now look, I am an intelligent man. I have thought very deeply about the religious life, and I am inclined to agree with you that some sort of change has to take place in a man before he can come into a saving relationship with God. In a sense he does have to be born when he is old, but how can this be? What are the methods and techniques? I am not suggesting that I need this radical change in my life, but as a matter of interest, if I did need it, how should I go about getting it?"

Nicodemus need not have looked far to find his answer. In the very house where he came to meet Jesus there were men of all ages who slept as peacefully as new-born babies because, in fact, they had died to their old lives and started life all over again as children of God: Matthew, Simon Peter, James and John and the others. Down in Jericho there was a man named Zacchaeus, a Jew who had been a tax-collector in the pay of the Roman government, an unscrupulous little "quisling", feared and hated by his compatriots, now living a life of astonishing integrity and kindliness, a life dedicated to making restitution to people whom he had defrauded. Up in Magdala there was a woman named Mary, of exciting loveliness, whose body had been her stock in trade saleable to the highest bidder, now living a life of astonishing purity and modesty, a life dedicated to the uplifting of the very people who had exploited and despised her. All of these were men and women who had been born when they were old, living proofs that human nature can be changed. Their secret? It stared Nicodemus in the face. These people had

47

met Jesus, someone who looked at them with the loving, understanding, forgiving eyes of God, whose own pure presence awakened their sleeping impulses to nobility and grandeur, and whose friendship drew them from the gutters of shame and cynicism and set their feet on a firm road of self-respect and hope.

How can a man be born when he is old? The story of Christianity answers that question of Nicodemus, because the story of Christianity might be gathered under the title of a book written by Harold Begbie, *Twice-Born Men*. Of many great Christians it could be said that they were born when they were old. In the fourth century a brilliant scholar from North Africa named Augustine, an ambitious and dissolute young man, turns from the fascinations around him and enters a quiet garden in Milan. There he feels a presence that directs him to read a passage of Scripture, and from that garden emerges a personality reborn, the most powerful and influential advocate of Christianity since St. Paul. In the thirteenth century a young Italian nobleman, later to be known as Francis, so gay, worldly and godless that his friends crowned him "King of the Revellers", turns his steps to a broken-down chapel on the outskirts of Assisi, and there he undergoes a change that issues in such a life of piety and Christian service that it stirs the hearts of many people and starts an evangelistic movement that sweeps through the cold, stuffy Church like a warm, fresh breath of springtime. "And what shall I more say; for the time would fail me to tell of . . . Ignatius Loyola, Martin Luther, John Wesley, William Wilberforce, Toyohiko Kagawa . . . the giants of the Faith," human personalities moving all in one direction who came under the transforming influence of Christ and of a sudden reversed themselves and moved in a different direction altogether.

How can a man be born when he is old? The question allows of no stereotyped answer. Indeed, we limit the Lordship and saving power of Christ by insisting that the conversion experience of rebirth should conform in everybody's life to an unvarying pattern. It savours of blasphemy when Christians of the ultra-pious variety set up a "conversion club", and stipulate as a requisite of membership that you should be able to fix the precise date and place of your second birth and celebrate its anniversary as publicly and glibly as you celebrate the anniversary of your first birth. It is true that a man may be "saved" in some sudden, spectacular experience, and that what the embryologists call "condensed evolution" may take place overnight in the human soul. It is also true, however, that some of the most lasting, earth-shaking Christian conversions have taken place quietly, almost imperceptibly and over a long period of time, so that only in retrospect, only by looking back, as you look down a mountain to see how far you have climbed, do you realize the extent of the change in your life.

So it happened to Thomas Chalmers, who in the eyes of his fellow-countryman, Carlyle, was the greatest Scotsman since John Knox. In his early years as a Divinity student Chalmers regarded the ministry superficially and even published an anonymous pamphlet to the effect that every minister ought to engage in secular work five days a week, since there was nothing in the service of the Church to claim all the time, all the devotion, all the intellectual vigour that a man possessed. The years passed, however, and Chalmers underwent a profound religious experience. He could not place this experience or date it. His rebirth was a gradual process, almost unconscious, but as he looked back he saw how all his great learning—mathematics, astronomy, political economy, philosophy, and a matchless eloquence—had been laid upon God's altar. Christ and the Church now claimed all of him there was. Addressing the Scottish General Assembly, he referred to his earlier pamphlet in these words: "Strangely blinded that I was! What, sir, is the object of mathematical science? Magnitude and the proportions of magnitude. But then, sir, I had forgotten two magnitudes. I thought not of the littleness of time. . . . I recklessly thought not of the greatness of eternity!"

The Master himself did not return a neat and simple answer to Nicodemus's question, "How can a man be born when he is old?" This thing is of God, and you do not prescribe human regulations for the operation of God's redeeming grace. "The wind blows where it wills, and you hear the sound of it, but you do not know whence it comes or whither it goes; so it is with everyone who is born of the Spirit." Of one thing only we can be certain: that just as surely as human nature can be changed by scientific stimuli, so for nineteen centuries people have come under the influence of Christ, under the stimulating, transforming influence of his friendship, and emerged from it totally different personalities with new loves and hates, new aims and purposes, prepared to contradict what they hitherto affirmed and to affirm what they hitherto contradicted. The Swiss psychiatrist, Carl Jung, declared that Christianity has added a new rung to the ladder of evolution. Christianity has produced on this earth a new creature who lives in a new way to which the natural man can no more attain than a crawling thing can fly; a creature whose way of life is so radically different from what it has left behind that we can describe it by no other term than "rebirth". So if the question be asked objectively, "How can a man be born when he is old?" it can be answered objectively, "He is born through friendship with Jesus Christ."

III

Suppose, however, that Nicodemus did not ask his question objectively. Suppose he asked it in yet another way—with passionate and profound yearning, as though this were the supreme secret, the pearl of great price which all his life he had been seeking and for which he would gladly exchange all his possessions. "Born again? Yes, this is what I want. I am tired of my life, tired of the person that I am now, tired of this losing battle between my ideals and my weak, sinful nature. I need rebirth. Spiritually I ought to die, to be erased from the book of life as though I had never been born. I know that if I am going to come into a right relationship with God, I shall have to go back to the beginning and start life all over again. You promise me that this is possible and I can see that it has happened to other people. But how does it happen to me, I who have come so far along the road of life, who have made so many irretrievable mistakes and whose failures and weaknesses have become fixed and congealed? How can a man be born when he is old?"

It is possible, you see, that a man may not really *want* this essential and constitutive experience in the Christian life, this almost painful and drastic conversion experience of rebirth. Imagine an arthritic cripple for thirty years bedridden in a charitable institution. One day there comes to his bedside a famed miracle-healer who looks compassionately at the invalid and says, "I shall make you well. I shall straighten those twisted limbs and restore life to that useless body. Rise from your bed and go out into the world!" Do you think he would accept the gift of healing, this paralytic who for thirty years has thrived on the misery of his own impotence, on self-pity and human sympathy? "No," he would reply, "I don't want to be healed. This hospital life is the only life I know. My friends are here. I don't know a soul on the outside. The world has changed since I came to this place. I could never adjust myself to it. I couldn't even get a job. Go away and leave me alone!" That is where second birth suffocates. Enslaving as it is, many people have become used to the misery of moral and spiritual paralysis, and though they may wish for the strength and the freedom that healing would bring, yet they have not the courage to accept it when it is offered to them.

Suppose, however, that a man does recognize as the great need of his life a change of character so decisive and drastic that it can only be described as a miracle of rebirth. The Apostle Paul believed that this *must* happen to us if we are going to enter our inheritance as sons of God; we must "put off the old nature with its practices, and put on the new nature, which is being renewed in knowledge after the image of its creator". The secret of this renewal is Jesus Christ. Writing to the Corinthians Paul says, "If any man be in Christ, he is a new creature; old things are passed away, behold, all things are become new." Paul has been telling his readers about the death and resurrection of Christ and of how they represent the operation of Divine grace in any man who by faith becomes a man in Christ. This had happened to Paul himself. He had died and had risen from the grave of his exclusive Jewish privileges. He was a different man now, no longer Saul the Pharisee, but Paul the Apostle. The Damascus Road virtually bisected his life. Before it he had persecuted Christianity; after it he became Christianity's most passionate propagator. Before it his soul had been crippled with a growing sense of guilt; after it his soul shone with the glory that is in Christ. The Apostle Paul stands before us as history's supreme example that through faith in Christ a man can be born when he is old.

Still we ask, *How* can a man be born when he is old? A brilliant graduate student of a theological school said to one of the older professors, "I am convinced that many people in our churches need the conversion experience of rebirth, and I should like to have it myself, but how do you do it?" The old professor looked at him and said, "You don't; *you* don't do it. *God* does it." The student shook his head and walked sadly away. You see, if the question were phrased, "Can we change human nature?" the answer would have to be "No". We have not the power to *recreate* life any more than we have the power to create life in the first place. Only a Power from above can release the power from within. Only a miracle of Divine grace can effect in our lives that death and resurrection from which we shall emerge new creatures capable of fulfilling our God-appointed destiny. And because the miracle has happened, because God in Christ has reached down into our human darkness, because there has taken place on this earth a Divine death and resurrection in which we can eternally share, therefore we can rephrase the question, "Can human nature be changed?" and our answer, our triumphant answer is "Yes".

"How can a man be born when he is old?" An old Dutch fable gives us our answer. There were three tulip bulbs named *No*, *Maybe* and *Yes*. They lived at the bottom of a bulb tin content to be round and fat, clothed in their silky, brown garments. When autumn came they fell to discussing the destiny of tulip bulbs. *No* said, "I shall stay in my snug corner of the bin. That there is any other life for tulip bulbs I deny. Besides, I am satisfied with things as they are." And he rolled over in the corner to sleep the winter away. *Maybe* said, "I am not satisfied with things as they are. I feel that there is a better life than the life I now have. I feel something inside me which I must achieve and I believe that I can achieve it." So he squeezed himself and squeezed himself and squeezed himself, and ended up in a fit of frustration. Then *Yes* said, "I have been told that we can do nothing of ourselves, but that the good Lord will fulfil our destiny if we put ourselves in his power." So one day a hand reached down into the bin groping for tulip bulbs. *Yes* gave himself to the hand and was buried in the earth throughout the long winter months. Meanwhile *No* and *Maybe* shrivelled away to uselessness, but when spring came, *Yes* burst forth with all the richness and loveliness of new life.

5

OUR HELPER IN THE CHRISTIAN LIFE

"Likewise the Spirit helps us in our weakness . . ."

(Romans 8:26)

IT WAS never intended that we should live the Christian life in our own strength. When the Risen Christ commissioned the disciples to be his witnesses and to carry the Gospel to "the uttermost parts of the earth", he did not leave them to their own resources, but promised them a superhuman strength. "You shall receive power when the Holy Spirit has come upon you." Christian Churches throughout the world celebrate the festival of Pentecost which marks the fulfilment of our Lord's promise in the descent of the Holy Spirit with power. We go behind the strange details of this almost bizarre event to the fact and the reality which it symbolizes—a community of frail, frightened, foolish men suddenly possessed by a Spirit greater than their own.

In a historic sense the Apostle Paul had not been present in the Upper Room. He had not heard the sound from heaven or felt the mighty wind or seen the tongues of fire. But Paul knew the truth of Pentecost. From that luminous moment when he surrendered his life to Christ on the Damascus Road, he was conscious of a Presence upholding, sustaining and guiding him in all situations. Christianity did not come easily to the great Apostle. He found it no spiritual tranquillizer, but a spiritual catalyst that threw his soul into turmoil and brought him to the brink of deep despair and discouragement. Never was a man more conscious of his own weakness, and of the gulf between all that he wanted to accomplish for Christ and all that he could, in fact, accomplish. Paul might have given up trying many times but for this marvellous fact: that whenever he reached a point in the Christian life where his own human resources failed, there surged through him a strength from beyond that nerved him and kept him on his feet. His own plans and purposes might peter out in frustration, but so long as he followed the will of Christ, the Spirit of Christ upheld him. He knew that from experience; therefore he wrote, "Likewise the Spirit helps us in our weakness."

It is hard to be a Christian. Christ never pretended otherwise. As someone has said, "He never hid his scars to win a disciple." Like Winston Churchill, who magnetized men during the war by his stark offer of "blood, toil, tears and sweat", so the Lord of Glory made it transparently clear that whoever would follow him must walk the way of a cross, the way of sacrifice, suffering and self-denial. It is hard to be a disciple of Jesus Christ, for his way is narrow and rocky and fraught with perils, and if we must walk it in our own strength then we shall not get very far before we sink to our knees exhausted or turn back discouraged. But the truth that we must ponder and possess is that we were never intended to walk the way of Christ in our own strength. We have a Helper in the Christian Life, the Holy Spirit; and this is no dead dogma, but a living truth about God, as men and women committed to Jesus Christ have actually experienced him. "Likewise the Spirit helps us in our weakness."

I

The Spirit helps us in our *intellectual weakness*. Generally speaking, we regard a man as acting perfectly within his rights if he switches from one profession to another, but for some unjust and illogical reason we attach a stigma to a man who leaves the ministry. I knew of such a person, fair to look upon, silver-tongued, brilliant in mind, magnetic in personality, a man with every ingredient for success except one thing. He could not reach a compromise with his doubts. Theologically it had to be all or nothing. He belonged to a conservative Church which held a fairly orthodox creed, and though he had consulted the scholars and exhausted all his great mental resources in the study of theology, yet he found that on certain basic doctrines he still stumbled, and one Sunday morning he shocked his large congregation by saying, "I don't know what I believe and I don't believe half of what I say. I have no alternative, therefore, but to leave the ministry."

We admire this man's moral honesty, and yet we wonder if he had not made the mistake of trying to go it alone. After all, he had set for himself an impossible task. No man can ever hope to understand the whole truth about God, simply because the finite mind cannot fully comprehend the Infinite. Who would think of attempting to cram a university education into the mind of an elementary school child? No less absurd is the assumption that we must swallow the whole body of Christian dogma in one gulp. Even to the disciples, tutored as they were by intimate fellowship with him, Jesus said in the Upper Room, "I have many things to say to you, but you cannot bear them now." Divine truth comes gradually; it comes only to the mind that develops and expands to receive it. "When the Spirit of truth comes, he will guide you into all the truth," he will be your permanent tutor in the Christian life.

In the Book of Acts we learn that the religious authorities marvelled at the wisdom and power of the disciples who, as they said, were "uneducated, common men". It has always been a source of mystery that people with comparatively little formal education should sometimes possess a profound understanding of Christian truth, and it allows of but one explanation, namely, that God himself has given it to them. Such people seem endowed with a spiritual sixth sense, a direct line of communication with the Eternal that eludes some of the most competent theologians, and that is what is meant by the Holy Spirit—*God within us recognizing God above.* As Martin Luther once said, "The simple scullery maid with the Holy Spirit can know more of God than the greatest scholar without the Holy Spirit."

John Keats wrote poetically about the thrill he experienced when first he read Chapman's translation of Homer. He compared it to that of an explorer who discovers a new continent or an astronomer when a new planet swims into his field of vision. Such thrilling discovery comes to the man who pursues the knowledge of God with the help of God's Holy Spirit. Some truth which has been nothing more than a dead doctrine suddenly comes alive and breathes into his consciousness with a meaning that changes the whole of life. In a moment of solitude or in a service of worship, familiar and almost hackneyed passages of Scripture become as the Voice of God speaking directly to our condition. Through the years the great doctrines of the faith, one by one, shed their academic dust and become precious and meaningful as an explanation of the truth about God. We do not acquire such knowledge; it is given to us, given by the Spirit of God helping us in our weakness.

II

The Spirit helps us in our *devotional weakness*. There is nothing more difficult in the Christian life than the discipline of prayer. Our very physical weaknesses impede us. Sleep overcomes us as it overcame the disciples in Gethsemane. "Could ye not watch with me one hour?" Jesus asked sadly. Then he added, "The spirit indeed is willing but the flesh is weak." Nor do we know how to pray as we ought. We kneel awkwardly, groping for suitable phrases, but the words die on our lips. Even if we do manage to articulate our longings, we are not at all sure that anybody hears them. So often our prayers have been unanswered. From the secret place we emerged as perplexed, as anxious and as crushed as we entered. We felt foolish and disillusioned, voicing our needs to a dull, unanswering silence, and many times we were tempted to end this pious mockery and give up praying altogether.

"The Spirit helps us in our weakness." At the very least we can say that the Spirit of God helps us to pray in spite of our doubt and discouragement. Something keeps drawing us back again to the secret place, even though there seems to be no one and nothing there, and many a man in a moment of extremity has been driven to his knees as if by some Unseen Force. Paul, however, speaks of a more profound

57

sense in which the Spirit of God assists our prayer life. "We do not know how to pray as we ought," yet there are times when petitions of sublime spiritual insight pour from our lips almost as though Another were speaking through us. I never reflect upon this truth without thinking of a humble man who tilled the soil, a Church Elder in one of my mission fields. He had almost no formal education. His grammar was atrocious. He possessed the most limited vocabulary. Sometimes, however, at my request, he stood before the congregation and said, "Let us pray"; and the language of devotion flowed from him like a symphony, eloquent and majestic, that fairly transported us to the gate of Heaven. Something possessed him, then, something speaking through him, *God within appealing to God above.*

Still more profoundly the Spirit of God helps us in our prayer weakness. "We do not know how to pray as we ought," writes Paul, and W. E. Orchard gives expression to that weakness in his classic of devotion, "O God, forgive the poverty, the pettiness, the childish folly of our prayers. . . . So often we pray for that which is already ours, neglected and unappropriated; so often for that which can never be ours; so often for that which we must win ourselves; and then labour endlessly for that which can only come to us in prayer." "We do not know how to pray as we ought." But, says Paul, "the Spirit Himself intercedes for us with sighs too deep for words"; and Dr. Orchard adds, "Listen not to our words, but to the groanings that cannot be uttered; hearken not to our petitions, but to the crying of our need." It is a daring thought that when we go down on our knees before God we are not alone. We have a Helper in the prayer-life, God within us appealing to God above, One who voices not the form of our petitions, but the unuttered substance of our needs and desires, and to these the Father in Heaven gives heed.

III

The Spirit helps us in our *moral weakness.* Who has not been discouraged by his failure to measure up morally? Someone has said that modern man is not worried about his sins, but the truth is that if we are morally serious and earnest at all we shall be more troubled about our misdeeds and failures than about anything else in the world. We know what Christ requires of us and that in every situation there is a Christian thing to do, a Christian way to react, a Christian word to say, a Christian decision to make; and we know how weak we have been, how dismally we have muffed our Christianity, how lamentably we have failed our Lord.

Can it be, however, that here again we have made the mistake of trying to go it alone? Christianity is not a system of ethics but a Gospel, the good news of something that happened and that still happens. The New Testament, especially the writings of Paul, sets forth the great Christian virtues not as something that we accomplish but as something that God accomplishes through us. "But the fruit of the Spirit is love, joy, peace, longsuffering, gentleness, goodness, faith, meekness, temperance." Read again that earthy and realistic breakdown of love into its component parts in the thirteenth chapter of First Corinthians. Moffatt translates it: "Love is very patient, very kind. Love knows no jealousy; love makes no parade, gives itself no airs, is never rude, never selfish, never irritated, never resentful; love is never glad when others go wrong, love is gladdened by goodness, always slow to expose, always eager to believe the best, always hopeful, always patient." It is not an ideal that the Apostle holds before us—for who would be sufficient for these things?—but a gift, the supreme gift of God's Holy Spirit, *God within us rendering obedience to God above*. We cannot cultivate it, but we can pray for it; we cannot achieve it, but we can receive it.

How dramatically we see that illustrated in the lives of the saints! When Francis of Assisi surrendered himself completely to Christ, he knew that henceforth he must regard his fellow-creatures, even the most repulsive of them, through the loving eyes of Christ. But how could he do it? How could he love the lepers, those uncared-for outcasts of humanity rotting to death in their colonies? One day he met a leper crying for alms. Francis was about to spur his horse when fear and disgust gave way to the strangest feeling. Something within impelled him to dismount, walk up to the leper, give him an alms, then slowly and deliberately press the man's rotten flesh against his lips. Francis had discovered by experience the doctrine of the Holy Spirit, the truth that no man has to live the Christian life in his own strength; once he puts himself in the way of Christ, the Spirit of Christ helps him in his weakness.

IV

The Spirit helps us in our *redemptive weakness*. Perhaps the most serious source of discouragement in the Christian life is the suspicion that we are really not Christians at all. We have always been aware that vital Christianity adds up to more than correct theology, more than devotional discipline, more than moral magnitude. We have a vague knowledge that something is supposed to happen inside us, something radical and redemptive that changes our personalities and makes us new creatures with new loves and hates, new aims and purposes. We have read about it and seen it in other people—Paul himself changed from persecutor to apostle, Wesley from pedant to evangelist, Kagawa from libertine to saint. What our Lord said to Nicodemus pounds on the back of our brain, "Except a man be born again, he cannot see the Kingdom of God," and we know in a moment that we have not been born again, not become new creatures in Christ. We have thought about this redemption experience, perhaps even longed for it and reached out for it, but we have to be honest with ourselves and admit that whatever is supposed to happen to a man when he becomes a vital Christian has not happened to us.

Once more, perhaps, we have made the mistake of trying to go it alone. We have relied too much upon ourselves, as though a saving relationship with God were something which we could achieve, and in our failure to achieve it we have made ourselves miserable with frustration. In his struggle to be at peace with God Martin Luther ran the whole gamut of the Roman Catholic penitential system, engaged in every conceivable discipline, performed every good work and scourged his body and soul, but his sense of imperfection and futility, of the unbridgeable gulf between his own sinfulness and God's holiness, issued in a physical illness that brought him to the brink of death. Almost in desperation he searched the Scriptures, and one day his eye lighted on a verse as though reading it for the first time, "The just shall live by faith." In a flash it came upon Luther that the secret of redemption, of a saving relationship with God, lies not in anything that we can do, but in our willingness to rely upon what God has done for us in Jesus Christ. "The just shall live by faith."

There are two factors in a vital redemptive experience. There is God's gracious act in Christ, and there is man's faith by which he responds to that act, faith that means belief and trust and obedience. "By grace are ye saved, through faith; and that—*even that*—not of yourselves: it is the gift of God." The grace of God did not end with the Cross, or with the Risen Christ appearing to his disciples and ascending to heaven on the clouds of glory. In that timeless event known as Pentecost God gives another manifestation of his grace, less visible but no less real, in the descent of his Holy Spirit with power. Not only does God act for our salvation in Christ, but he himself stirs up within us the precious gift of faith whereby we shall know that Christ is our Saviour and Lord. Even our response to God's Christ is not essentially our own work, but the work of the Holy Spirit impelling us to believe that what Christ has done he has done for us, impelling us to trust Christ and obey him. As Paul writes, "No one can say 'Jesus is Lord,' except by the Holy Spirit." That is what we mean by the Holy Spirit—the awakening power whereby we realize our redemption, *God within us responding to God above*.

Once in a long while something happens that vindicates our faith in the Church's ministry. Recently I noticed a striking young man teaching a group of boys in a Sunday School class. I knew him well a decade ago, an engaging personality, morally upright, interested but not concerned about the Church, and not a particularly convinced Christian; hardly a religious man. But now he was different. He looked different. His face had a radiance, his eyes a lustre, and his very bearing a quality of gentleness and dedication. You could see that the Church had become the most important thing in his life. For one brief moment he took me aside and spoke words that I could scarce believe, words that played music on the strings of my soul. He said, "I have had an experience of God since you last saw me. It came one afternoon as I sat alone in my house. God was beside me and I knew it. I could feel his presence filling my whole being. I broke down and wept like a child, and when I rose to my feet I knew that I was a changed man. Everything pointed in a different direction, and I knew that from that moment I should have to walk in that direction. Can you explain it for me?" Yes, I could explain it. I could explain it as that for which all of us must pray unceasingly, the awakening power of the Holy Spirit, God within us responding to God above.

6

THE FIRST MILE

"If any one forces you to go one mile, go with him two miles."
(St. Matthew 5:41)

PERHAPS OUR Lord said that on a day when he saw
one of his fellow-countrymen tagging along like a beast
of burden behind a burly Roman soldier. That was the
law of the land. Any Roman could arrest a Jew at any hour
of the day or night and compel him to carry his pack for a
distance of one mile. How bitterly the Jews must have hated
this symbol of social degradation, and how tempted they
must have been to spit in the faces of their arrogant over-
lords! They obeyed, however; they had no alternative if
they valued their lives. So we can imagine the shocked
reaction of the disciples when Jesus let fall this little bomb-
shell, "If any one forces you to go one mile, go with him two
miles. . . . Don't just be bullied by your enemy. You take
the initiative and help the man instead; then you, not he,
will be in control of the situation."

"If any one forces you to go one mile, go with him two
miles." Somehow this concept of the second mile expresses
the Christian philosophy of life. What does it mean to be a
Christian except that one does go a second mile?—he goes
beyond the limits of necessity and compulsion and voluntarily shoulders heavier burdens for the sake of Christ. There
is a plus factor in essential Christianity, something that lifts
the Christian above the best non-Christian. Jesus said to the
disciples, "Except your righteousness exceed that of the
Scribes and Pharisees, you will in no wise enter the Kingdom
of Heaven." And how often he applied this principle to some
specific moral issue. For example, when Peter asked him,
"How often shall my brother sin against me and I forgive

him, till seven times?" Jesus replied, "No, that calculated behaviour belongs only to the realm of civilized decency. You belong to the realm of God where forgiveness has no limits. Not seven times, but seventy times seven."

There has been a great deal written and said about the second mile of Christian discipleship, but I cannot recall ever reading a book or hearing a sermon about the first mile. Surely this is the more demanding stage in life's journey. There is, after all, something enjoyable, or at least morally satisfying, about doing things, even unpleasant things, because you *want* to do them; but it is very hard to enjoy the things that you *have* to do, those burdens and responsibilities that you carry whether you like them or not. Any first century Jew commandeered by a Roman soldier would tell you that the difficult thing was getting started, swallowing his pride, shouldering the heavy pack and serving his enemy knowing that he had no choice but to serve him. Once he had surmounted that obstacle, the very momentum carried him forward, and he could, if he wanted, continue his journey sustained by a certain sense of exhilaration. The most difficult thing about the Christian life is always to get started on it—not to exceed the law's demands but to fulfil the law's demands, not to pass the best non-Christian in the race but simply to catch up with the best non-Christian. Even as Christians we must walk that first long mile of grinding necessity and bitterly humiliating compulsion, and for this we need all the impulses, all the encouragement, all the resources which our religious faith affords.

Once I ventured to speak flatteringly of a man who had distinguished himself in his line of work and had been the recipient of many honours. Without jealousy, but quite matter-of-factly, a colleague of his remarked, "Of course, you must remember that the very nature of his work brings it under the spotlight of publicity." He went on, "I think many of us are just as competent and faithful, but because we do unglamorous work, nobody pays much attention to us." You can apply that to the Christian life and say that people who make conspicuous sacrifices for the sake of Christ do eventually win the admiration of their fellows. Everybody notices the great Christian, the heroic missionary or the dedicated social worker or the hard-working minister who so obviously walks the second mile of Christian service. It is encouraging to be noticed in this way, and you feel upheld also by a sometimes un-Christian sense of moral superiority. But nobody applauds the man who for Christ's sake walks the first mile. That man, though he may struggle hard, is considered to be simply a decent, respectable, law-abiding citizen. Nor does he himself feel superior, because, like the slave in our Lord's parable who came home from the fields at nightfall to wait on his master's table, he knows himself to be an unprofitable servant who has done only that which it was his duty to do.

This may explain why some Christians attempt the rather impossible trick of leaping over the first mile and beginning their journey at the second. These are the people who fulfil life's extras but not its requirements, who embrace the ideals and neglect the hard realities, who make voluntary sacrifices for Christ and fail to do what Christ demands. These are the people like Mrs. Jellyby who knit woollen sweaters for the natives of Equatorial Africa while her own son, Peepy, shivers in the cold. These are the head-table guests at a dinner who become noted for the generosity with which they support any worthwhile enterprise, the "front-men"—you have them in every Church—who invariably make their appearance at the last stages of the enterprise after the donkey work has all been done.

I remember a man who was an expert at walking the second mile. My wife and I met him in Geneva as we were coming away from the World Council of Churches office. He was a fascinating character, gracious and affable, and when he learned our identity he invited us to have lunch with him at his home. A free-lance journalist, he submits articles to newspapers all over the world, and for years he has been organizing an endless succession of voluntary inter-national committees to deal with the problems obstructing world peace. At that time he was busy with the Swiss Com-mittee for the Reunification of Germany. The only trouble is that he does not earn a living at it. His wife—we never met

WHAT IS A CHRISTIAN?

the long-suffering lady—works as a nurse in a nearby prison hospital in order to pay the rent, provide food for overseas guests and finance her husband in his full-time hobby. She has to take minor precautions such as keeping the telephone locked in a cupboard in order to prevent her world-citizen husband from making long-distance calls to New York or Hong Kong. This charming fellow was an expert at travelling the second mile; somehow he had forgotten to walk the first mile.

Our society would move closer to the Kingdom of God if many Christians forgot the idealism of the second mile and simply fulfilled the hard realities of the first mile. Consider that truth in relation to certain areas of life. The home is an area of the first mile and our duty as parents and children not something meritorious that we accept voluntarily, but something that God and society have a right to expect of us. Nothing sounds quite as hollow as the parent who accuses her children of ingratitude and tries to shame them by saying, "Your father and I sacrifice a great deal to give you a good education and provide you with so many nice things." The obvious retort is—what else are parents for? Our children did not ask to be born. We brought them into the world and we have, therefore, certain basic obligations toward them. To be sure, nothing seems more unglamorous and thankless than being the slave of your own family, but serving your own family is the first mile of Christian parenthood, and if more parents walked it cheerfully, the home would be a saner and more stable institution than it is today.

Everybody admires Mrs. Brown. She caters for dinners at the church, serves on all the neighbourhood committees and organizes charity campaigns for her club. Friends say that she should go into politics. But talk to her family; they would like to get her back into the home. Her husband wishes that she would do more catering for the dining-room table. Her daughters would like to get in committee with their mother about some of their own problems. Her aged father, now a bed-ridden invalid, wishes that she would organize a bit of charity in his direction. Mrs. Brown walks the second mile of Christian idealism and service but she forgets to walk the

first mile of Christian responsibility. It recalls the words of
Paul to Timothy, "If anyone does not provide for his
relatives, and especially for his own family, he has disowned
the faith and is worse than an unbeliever."

Daily work is another area of the first mile, and Christians
ought not to forget that when they come together in conferences to talk about the dignity and vocation of labour.
In recent years the Church has been so concerned with
spiritualizing the secular professions that we may have
forgotten that even as secular professions they are still areas
of Christian obedience. Before the floor-sweeper, the mechanic, the teacher or the civil servant begins turning his work
into a Christian ministry, he has first of all to do a good job
as a floor-sweeper, a mechanic, a teacher, a civil servant.
That is the first mile, and right now our society needs desperately to be shown what it means to travel the first mile.
In North America the steel unions have announced that they
intend asking for a thirty-two hour week. It takes the average
minister twenty hours to prepare a sermon, and he usually
preaches two sermons a Sunday, and preaching comprises
only part of his work. Thirty-two hours! Why not go the
whole way and demand a guaranteed annual wage for simply
being alive? These days we hear too much about the right
to work and not enough about the duty to work. There was
an office manager who complained that one of his employees
spent too much time telephoning and writing letters about
church affairs during business hours. Being a bit of a cynic,
he said, "You Christians might be more honest if you were
less religious and gave a fair day's work for a fair day's
pay."

Jesus in his Sermon on the Mount told the disciples that,
as followers of him, they must go beyond the first mile of
common morality; yet we know and predict that our society
would be re-made from top to bottom if men and nations
today would travel the first mile of common morality. "You
have heard that it was said to the men of old, 'You shall not
kill' . . . (first mile). But I say to you that every one who is
angry with his brother shall be liable to judgment" (second
mile). Surely, however, the second mile begins only where

the first mile ends. How shall we enter the area of more civilized and polite relationships as long as we invest our money and our best brains in creating weapons of mass killing? "You have heard that it was said, 'You shall not commit adultery' . . . (first mile). But I say to you that every one who looks at a woman lustfully has already committed adultery with her in his heart" (second mile). Here again no one would deny that the Christlike ideal is a chaste and guileless imagination, but anyone engaged in the sorrowful business of healing guilty consciences knows that untold damage would be avoided if young people simply disciplined themselves and egotistical men were faithful to their wives. "You have heard that it was said to the men of old, 'You shall not swear falsely' . . . (first mile). But I say to you, do not swear at all. . . . Let what you say be simply Yes or No" (second mile). I am all for swearing, however, when it means the taking of oaths and abiding by them. Before human problems can be resolved by mere verbal agreements, the human race needs to recover a fundamental integrity. "You have heard that it was said, 'You shall love your neighbour and hate your enemy' . . . (first mile). But I say to you, Love your enemies. . . ." Here is the ultimate in Christlikeness, the second mile of Christian love, but the trouble with many of us is that we have not yet travelled the first mile. Our problem is self-centredness; we love only ourselves. The world is full of people who bear no malice towards us, who long to be our neighbours, but we care nothing for them; we do not even know that they exist. If we do not love those who love us, how shall we ever learn to love those who hate us?

It takes peculiar qualities of mind and heart to take a person *beyond* the first mile. No one exceeds the limits of duty and obligation unless something stronger than himself drives him. The Roman soldier, when he commanded a Jew to carry his pack for a mile, did not expect him to keep going after they had travelled the prescribed distance. He knew that the miserable fellow would probably drop the burden as though it were contaminated and walk away with a look of hatred on his face. It would have jolted the burly pagan if, as he turned and said not unkindly, "I'll take it now," the reply came, "It's all right. You look tired. I shall carry it a bit further." He would assume that either the Jew had suffered sunstroke, or else that he was driven by some inner impulse which he, the Roman, did not understand. Only one thing would surprise him more than a Jew who offered to go a second mile, and that would be a Jew who walked the first mile without a look of resentment and hatred written all over his face; one who did only what was commanded of him, but did it ungrudgingly and cheerfully. That also would indicate peculiar qualities of mind and heart. We go the second mile of religion because we have the resources of religion, but let us not forget that those same resources provide the impulse for the first mile.

There is the sense of *Divine empowerment*; it not only brings us through the crises and makes us adequate for life's extras; it gives us the spiritual stamina, the patience, the self-control, the endurance for life's everyday common duties. That verse from Isaiah, "They that wait upon the Lord shall renew their strength. They shall mount up with wings as eagles, they shall run and not be weary, they shall walk and not faint"—follows the realistic order of climax, because the spirit needs renewal not so much for the sprints and flights of life, as for the long, humdrum days of plodding necessity. Renewal comes from God.

H. E. Fosdick tells of a woman who, comparatively young, was left a widow with five children. By careful management she saw all of them through college. One son became President of a great railway system, another became President of a university, another became a leading pioneer in his field of medical research. That mother was an extraordinary personality; she had neither the strength nor the opportunity to walk the second mile of life, but she walked the first mile with dignity and courage. She died in her ninety-sixth year, and on the day of her funeral the children said that they had never seen her impatient or distraught to the point of giving up, even in the most troubled times. It was the university president who declared that no-one could understand his mother who did not understand the meaning of faith; her faith, he said, was a force that released radiance and power.[1]

The sense of *Divine approval* sustains us for the first mile. It is true that when we distinguish ourselves morally and make voluntary sacrifices for Christ we are upheld by the sense of sharing in something great and important, but we must not assume that the ordinary duties of life at home, at work and in our daily relationships have no eternal significance. In our Lord's parable the man with two talents received exactly the same approbation in exactly the same words as the five-talent man, "Well done, good and faithful servant; you have been faithful over a little, I will set you over much; enter into the joy of your master." For the things we *have* to do, the burdens and responsibilities that we *must* carry whether we like them or not, we have the highest impulse, the impulse of obedience to God. We are doing what God requires of us, and as we do our best, so we have his approval.

Leslie Weatherhead tells the story of a sixteen-year-old girl who lay dying in a great city hospital. She had literally caved in under the exhausting responsibility of running the house and bringing up her orphaned brothers and sisters. Her face was white and drawn. Her hands were rough and stained with the hard work of the years. To her bedside came an unfortunately narrow-minded church worker who questioned the patient about religion. Had she been confirmed? No! Had she been baptized? No! Had she gone to Sunday School? No! Had she attended church? No, she had never had time for that. The lady visitor took a very serious view of the situation. "What will you do," she asked, "when you die and have to tell God that?" The girl made an answer that is too sublime for comment. Very quietly she whispered the words, "I shall show him my hands."

A sense of *Divine companionship* sustains us as we walk the first mile. Let us never make the mistake of looking for Christ only when we engage in what seem like religious acts of great sacrifice. Remember that the Son of God, before he himself set foot upon the road that took him to a Cross, spent years of his life as a village carpenter toiling for the support of his

[1] Harry Emerson Fosdick, *Riverside Sermons* (Harper and Brothers, Publishers, New York 1958), p. 113

family. He, too, walked that first mile of grinding necessity and bitterly humiliating compulsion. It is this Carpenter of Nazareth, this very ordinary man who rose from the dead and appeared to his disciples, who meets us now when we wash dishes at the kitchen sink or try to get along with people or express a point of view that is truthful and good. Christ does not postpone his presence until we have entered the second mile of Christian discipleship. He comes to our side the moment we acknowledge and obey him; he walks with us from the very beginning of the first mile, and he accompanies us down that difficult road which he himself knows so well.

7

A PLEA FOR SIMPLER LIVING

"The Lord preserveth the simple . . ."

(Psalm 116:6)

THE ONE hundred and sixteenth Psalm is an expression of overwhelming praise to God. See how the poet begins, "I love the Lord, because he hath heard my voice and my supplications. Because he hath inclined his ear unto me, therefore will I call upon him as long as I live." God had wrought a marvellous miracle in this man's life. He had delivered his soul from death, his eyes from tears and his feet from falling. And now the Psalmist simply cannot articulate the gratitude that rises within him. "What shall I render unto the Lord for all his benefits toward me?" One thing is sure: he will make his thanksgiving a public act; he will go into the Lord's house and pay his vows in the presence of the congregation. He wants to share with all the world this tremendous spiritual experience; he wants people to know how available is the power of God to those who call upon him in their affliction. And he wants them to know the kind of life that offers free and untrammelled access to the Divine mercy and grace. "The Lord preserveth the simple."

This ancient Hebrew poet speaks a timely word to our situation. Life in our mechanized, urbane society has become very complicated, and many of us find ourselves baffled by the problem of how to live in this complexity which we did not create and cannot control. We are serious-minded people concerned with living our lives effectively, using our energies constructively, performing our allotted tasks fruitfully and creatively. In our reflective moments each might be asking a question like this: With one life to live on this earth, how can I live it significantly and victoriously? How can I make the greatest possible contribution to the common good and achieve the highest happiness for myself?

There are many people who have wrestled with that problem in the deep places of the soul, and whose experience corroborates the Psalmist's conviction that an effective life, a life so in tune with the Infinite that God can get through to it with grace and power, is essentially a simple life, a life which has been consciously and deliberately simplified. "The Lord preserveth the simple."

The truth finds expression in a parable. One of my pastorates was in that beautiful strip of land known as "the garden of Canada", the Niagara Peninsula where peaches grow abundantly. Much to my disappointment, our own heavily laden tree yielded miserably dwarfed fruit little larger than plums. When I complained to some of the local growers, they laughed and said, "You should have pruned the tree." I did so the following year, though it seemed a colossal waste to discard half-a-dozen healthy looking peaches for every one left on the branch. In late summer, however, the pruning process paid off, because the tree yielded fruit large and luscious. What is the moral? That life, when simplified, becomes more fruitful; that the secret of abundant living may very often lie in a conscious pruning process which, though it seems wasteful and perhaps difficult at the time, yields rich dividends in the harvest.

I

That means stripping life down to the essentials. The simple life is *an unburdened life*, a journey through this world of time and space where a man travels easily and swiftly because he travels light. It is a life controlled by the wisdom that distinguishes between necessity and luxury, a life unencumbered by excess baggage, taking what it requires for the journey and leaving behind what it can do without.

The modern gadgets and appliances at an exhibition or a motor show symbolize our materialistic civilization. Wistfully a man surveys the latest model car, lovingly a woman fondles an automatic dishwasher, and you can see in their eyes the burning flame of desire and hear them whispering softly, "If only I could afford this thing!" All of us have our hearts set on material things needed to complete our happiness. But do we need them, or have they become an obsession, aggravated by clever advertising methods and by our own insatiable greed?

Jesus enunciated a principle as relevant to the twentieth century as to the first. He said that "a man's life does not consist in the abundance of his possessions". Indeed, the Master issued a warning to the effect that a man might acquire many possessions, might gain the whole world and discover that in the process he has lost his essential humanity. Some months ago a wealthy man entertained me for dinner at his club. He has made money and made it quickly. Afterwards we went to his home, an impressive-looking mansion, richly furnished, with five bathrooms in it. Expensive mirrors entirely line the walls and ceilings of one of the bathrooms—a dubious asset! The corner of his library revolves like a "lazy susan", on the one side books which he has never read, on the other side a bar laden with all kinds of bottles. He showed me pictures of his beautiful country home, showed me his sports equipment and three new models of electric razor. "You have so much," I remarked. "Ah yes," he replied sadly, "but the trouble with having a lot of things is that you don't control them; they control you."

Frugality, living modestly even when one can afford to live more luxuriously, has ceased to be a virtue among us. Yet how sedulously some of the wealthiest and most successful men have practised it. Of John D. Rockefeller it was estimated that in 1913 his assets exceeded nine hundred million dollars, a fortune growing at the rate of one hundred dollars a minute. We are told, however, that this richest of all Americans was a simple man of plain tastes. He avoided flamboyant dress, never mentioned his wealth at home, loved to eat bread and milk and raw apples, abstained from drink, and conducted family worship every day. William Ewart Gladstone would hardly have fitted into "the convivial society" of our day. Though a wealthy man, he practised a frugality that irritated many of his friends. As Prime Minister he obstinately refused to do any political entertaining or to join any of the swankier clubs where important people meet one another. After putting through the Railway Act of 1844 which provided decent accommodation for third-class passengers, Gladstone made a point of often travelling third class himself—like Albert Schweitzer who says that he always travels third class because there is no fourth. Benjamin Jowett said of Gladstone that no one of such great simplicity had ever before been found in so exalted a station. Jowett might have looked across the Atlantic to Gladstone's American contemporary, Abraham Lincoln.

Not without reason did Francis of Assisi advocate voluntary poverty, believing that a man can travel to God only along the road of self-denial. When one of his disciples, having learned to read, expressed a desire for a Psalter of his own, Francis replied sternly, "After the Psalter thou wilt be covetous and desire to have a breviary also, and after thou hast a breviary thou wilt sit in a chair like a great prelate and say to thy brother, 'Fetch me the breviary'." Excess baggage impedes the soul's progress toward God. The simple life is an unburdened life, a life stripped down to the essentials. "The Lord preserveth the simple."

II

The simple life is also *an unpretentious life,* a life controlled by the wisdom that acknowledges its own limitations. This was the moral of a book popular a few years ago, Sloan Wilson's *The Man in the Gray Flannel Suit.* Goaded on by his employer, pressured by competitiveness, consumed by his own lust for money and power, the hero, Tom, drove himself like a machine, senseless of what success was costing him. Only by calling a halt to this mad process, only by a conscious decision to settle for something less pretentious, only by recognizing his limitations and courageously simplifying his ambitions did he at last work out his salvation, recover his poise, and hold his home together.

It is a hard lesson to learn, because life thrusts ambition

upon us; it compels us to struggle beyond our strength. Most of us, whether we like it or not, find ourselves caught up in a mad, competitive race for existence, like those six-lane super-highways where you have no choice but to keep your foot on the accelerator and travel at a breakneck speed mile after endless mile. To get ahead these days, some men work seven days a week and take their brief-cases home in the evenings; they never refuse a business invitation and never eat a relaxing meal; recreation they consider an indulgence and holidays a waste of time. One day, like a piece of stiff wire which has been flexed repeatedly and vigorously, they reach the fatigue limit and snap like a dry twig. Then it is that some kindly physician orders them to bed or refers them to a psychiatrist.

In one of the colleges of a great university a graduate student hanged himself in his lodgings. The porter found him after he had been dead several hours. It seems that for two years he had been working, without much progress, on a doctoral thesis, a lonely and discouraging exercise. You can usually single out the Ph.D. students in a university; they are chronic pessimists; they rarely admit that things are going well, they work by themselves, they know what it means to follow a line of thought for months and then scrap everything and start all over again. This thesis period is a highly abnormal period in one's education, and no man should tackle it unless he has infinite patience and nerves of steel. Unfortunately, this student had been deficient in those very qualities. "It was just too much for him," observed his supervisor; "we suggested that he abandon the Doctor's degree and settle for something less ambitious, but he was determined to go ahead at all costs."

We shall not glamorize mediocrity. It may well be that the timeliest word that can be spoken to this security-conscious generation is not a word to quench honest ambition but to stimulate it. Nevertheless, let us recall the question that we are asking: with one life to live on this earth, how shall we live it significantly and victoriously? How make it count to the full? We can be sure of this: that while we owe it to ourselves to achieve the highest within us, we shall never make a success of life—the whole of life, not just our daily work which is only one department of life—until we control our egotism and proclaim an armistice in the civil war between our ambitions and our limitations. Somewhere along the way we have to subject ourselves to the discipline of honest self-assessment; somewhere we have to cease living on the basis of what we should like to do and like to become, and begin living on the basis of what we can do and what we are. Somewhere we have to decide that the Creator has endowed us with just so much energy and just so much ability, and on the basis of these realities, not of some grandiose vision, make our contribution to the common good. "The Lord preserveth the simple."

III

We can go a step further and say that the simple life is *an uncrowded life*, a life controlled by the wisdom that knows how to distinguish between what is of primary and what is of secondary importance. Community life in any small village in North America usually centres in the general store, a combination post office, petrol station and emporium where merchandise of every variety, from drugs to drapery, from confectionery to hardware, bulges from the shelves, hangs from the ceiling and lies strewn about the floor. The general store symbolizes many lives, lives so cluttered with a variety of interests and obligations that any semblance of order and organization becomes physically impossible. Life in modern society is very overcrowded. We have to take on so much these days. No sooner do we move into a community than our professional status, our social obligations, our membership in this or that important organization put their claim upon us, and to none have we the courage to say "No". Before we know it, we are bowed down with burdens, crushed under committees, panting through a never-ending programme of meetings and appointments, too exhausted to do our work effectively, too busy to be good companions of our children, with no time at all for the enrichment of our own mind and spirit.

We had better make up our minds that the problem is not going to solve itself. Life has become hyper-organized, and no matter where we live, we shall not be able to unravel the complex pattern. Sometimes we conjure up unreal visions of chucking the whole business and going to live in the country; yet we know that if there is any answer at all, it will have to be found not outside the world's complexity, but within the world's complexity. We have to begin with ourselves, by house-cleaning our own overcrowded lives. Obviously life is too short to permit enjoyment of all the fascinations in this complicated world, therefore we need to exercise the conscious faculty of choice; we need to distinguish between what is of primary and what is of secondary importance. To each imperious claim on our time and energy we need to apply some wise principle of selection such as this: I want to do this thing and perhaps I ought to do it, but will it make any difference six months from now? Our popularity may suffer for it, but not our personal effectiveness, not the calibre of our daily work, and not the health of our body or the sanity of our mind. Many a man, confined to bed by a heart attack, has thought soberly in the quiet hours of how unnecessary were some of his hurried business trips—a telephone call or a letter would have done just as well; and how unessential were the luncheons and banquets he attended—his absence would not have been noticed. We pay a high price, sometimes, to get wise.

A minister called at the home of a lady in his parish. She had been a beautiful woman until a sudden decline in health caused her to grow abnormally thin and pale. Friends at the church whispered that she might be suffering from some organic ailment, perhaps a malignant disease, so they urged the minister to pay a pastoral visit. She sat there, her hands trembling, her eyes brimming with tears. "I feel ashamed of myself," she burst out, "I am so depressed all the time, so irritable with the children, such a worry to my husband. We have to attend a cocktail party tonight, and I just dread the thought of going." "Do you have to go to this party?" the minister asked. "Oh yes," she replied, "these things go with my husband's position. We have no choice. Some weeks he and I never have a single night at home." The minister told this lady that he had faced a similar problem in his own overcrowded life and had realized that if he hoped to preserve his strength of body and soul, he must prune the tree radically and take the consequences. He recommended a book which had helped him greatly, *A Testament of Devotion*, by the Quaker, Thomas Kelly, especially its chapter on "The Simplification of Life". She read this book, she took it seriously, she reorganized her life on the basis of it, and the phrase became almost a form of greeting at the church door on Sunday mornings. "How goes the simplification of life?" she would ask the minister in the days after beauty's radiance had set its bloom on her cheeks again.

Of course, the problem is a spiritual one. Jesus told his first parable about a sower casting seed into four kinds of soil; and it requires little imagination to see that most of us fit Soil Type Three. We are not hardened or impervious to the Gospel. The Word of God strikes real rootage in our lives. The only trouble is that it does not have a chance to grow. The weeds and thorns of competing interests—our marriage to the golf course or a summer home, our membership in this club or that lodge, our childish pursuit of some hobby, our passion to make money, our desire to be identified with a particular social group, or even our idolizing of home and family—these things grow more rapidly than the life of the spirit and eventually strangle it. "Other seed fell among thorns." Even the most amateur gardener knows that ground has to be cultivated and weeds torn up by the roots if good plants are to come to fruition. Likewise the soul will never grow upwards to God unless we make room for it to grow, simplifying life, tearing out many interests, activities and obligations which, though not wrong in themselves, are of secondary importance in the eternal perspective. "The Lord preserveth the simple."

IV

We can say also that the simple life is *an unhurried life*, a

79

life controlled by the wisdom of slowing down occasionally. There is nothing attractive about these new greeting cards that measure nine inches tall and four inches across and specialize in a pathetically unfunny humour. One of them, however, caught my attention, because it conveyed in bold type the words of a modern beatitude: "Blessed is he that goeth around in circles, for he shall become a big wheel."

It is a sad but accurate commentary on twentieth-century life that business should be identified with busyness, and success with feverish haste. We make a fetish of our hectic activity. We admire the man who is always dashing off to keep an appointment; we assume that he must be a successful man. And such a time-conscious people we are, always trying to save time or make time. A recent book pokes fun at us by describing a man who one morning used two shaving brushes instead of one and saved seventeen seconds. Next morning he used two razors instead of one and saved additional seconds. On the third morning he lost two minutes patching up his chin which had been sliced by the second razor. "Blessed is he that goeth around in circles . . ."

What an illusion to believe that the faster we move the more we accomplish, for the truth is that those who move at a measured, even leisurely pace very often lead the most productive lives. Have you ever wondered why it is that some people manage to get done in the average day so much more than others are able to do? Indefatigable, dynamic, prolific in their labour, they seem to accomplish the work of ten lifetimes in one. Yet they move with such poise, always relaxed, never dissipating their strength, always human beings, never machines. It is constantly revealing, in reading the biographies of such men, to discover how many of them found their secret in the simple art of slowing down occasionally. They paused. They took time to think; and from these periods of apparent inactivity drew rich resources of mind and spirit that gave purpose and direction to their labours.

In his biography of Leonardo da Vinci, Antonio Vallenten dwells upon the simplicity of the da Vinci family. They were all professional people, urbane and prosperous, yet they led a simple, routine existence. They worked hard and had few wants. As the biographer says, "They liked nourishing, uncomplicated food, avoided ostentation in dress, and economized on the pleasures of the moment for the sake of the morrow." In Milan you can visit the little Church of Santa Maria delle Grazie, where Leonardo painted his famous canvas of the Last Supper and where he spent many hours meditating in the cloister. The monks, it seemed, resented these idle periods. They expected something altogether different, a finished production in record time. Indeed, the good Fathers suspected the artist of taking advantage of his contract, so they remonstrated with him, but Leonardo answered, "When I pause the longest, I make the most telling strokes with my brush."

At this point, no doubt, the members of my congregation might retort sarcastically, "Look who's talking!" It is true that few professional men these days lead so hectic and complicated an existence as does the average minister. Like not-so-well-oiled machines we are on the go morning, afternoon and evening for seven days a week, except during vacation, and even then some of us have not the sense to take a holiday. Men of God, as we are supposed to be, we can scarcely find time to say our prayers. There is one prayer, though, which I say many times. I keep it prominently displayed on my office desk. It goes like this:

"Slow me down, Lord! Ease the pounding of my heart by the quieting of my mind. Steady my hurried pace with a vision of the eternal reach of time. Give me, amidst the confusion of my day, the calmness of the everlasting hills. Break the tension of my nerves and muscles with the soothing music of the singing streams that live in my memory. Help me to know the magical, restoring power of sleep. Teach me the art of taking minute vacations—of slowing down to look at a flower, to chat with a friend, to pat a dog, to read a few lines from a good book. Remind me each day of the fable of the hare and the tortoise, that I may know that the race is not always to the swift; that there is more to life than increasing its speed. Let me look upward into the branches of the towering oak and know that it grew great and strong because it grew slowly and well. Slow me down, Lord, and inspire me to send my roots deep into the soil of life's enduring values that I may grow toward the stars of my greater destiny. . . ."

"The Lord preserveth the simple. . . ." Ponder this timely insight of an ancient Hebrew Psalmist—that a simple life, which means an unburdened, unpretentious, uncrowded and unhurried life, offers freest access to the grace and power of God. That is surely the testimony of the greatest life of all, a life poor in material possessions, free from all personal ambition, so uncrowded that it moved forward with singleness of purpose, so unhurried that it allowed time for whole nights in prayer—life reduced to utmost simplicity, yet life lived with supreme significance and in perfect harmony with God. In Jesus Christ, Child of Mary, Carpenter of Nazareth, God has revealed here on earth human life at its highest and best; he has shown us that the full, effective, God-empowered life is essentially a simple life, like a tree which, having been radically pruned, brings forth fruit large and luscious. "The Lord preserveth the simple."

8

A GOSPEL FOR THE MIDDLE-AGED

"... the destruction that wasteth at noonday."

(Psalm 91 :6)

IN EACH generation the Church alters its programme emphasis to meet the changing needs. A generation ago we poured our best brains and resources into the Christian education of our growing boys and girls. "We must do something for the young people" became the slogan in every congregation, a conviction fired by the example of Hitler's Youth Movement and by the awareness that the children of today will shape tomorrow's world and Church. In more recent years the pendulum has swung to the opposite extreme, our concern directed to a group long neglected— the "senior citizens", those retired warriors of yesterday's Church but for whose devotion and sacrifice there would be no Christian heritage to bequeath to our growing boys and girls.

Not for a moment should we question the legitimacy or the importance of such emphases. Youth does have its peculiar problems occasioned by physical development, intellectual growth and emotional upheaval. Youth is a plastic, impressionable period, a time for making life's crucial decisions, which means that the Church in its ministry to young people has an opportunity that it will never have again. Maturity has its problems too. Nobody likes to grow old, however gracefully they manage to do it. With age come the anxiety and worry occasioned by physical infirmity, economic stringency, adjustment to inactivity, and often by the loneliness of being neglected and unwanted. We Christians have, under the constraint of love, a very special obligation to those in our fellowship who have reached life's eventide.

May I suggest, however, that the most pressing spiritual needs make themselves felt neither in the morning of youth, nor in the eventide of maturity, but in the noonday of middle-age? The Psalmist sings of "the destruction that wasteth at noonday". Of course, we have to define middle-age, and I find that it becomes an arbitrary designation, movable as one grows older. Dante, you remember, begins his *Divine Comedy*:

> "In the midway of this our mortal life
> I found me in a gloomy wood, astray
> Gone from the path direct . . ."

This "midway" period Dante fixes at the thirty-fifth year of his age. Human life he compares to an arch or bow, the highest point of which occurs, in those well-framed by nature, at their thirty-fifth year. Fix it where you may, however, middle-age is a critical time in life. Nobody wants to admit that they have reached it, and nobody wants to admit that they have passed it. From a purely materialistic point of view, one's thirty-fifth year, or thereabouts, brings the greatest economic responsibility. The child draws a baby bonus. Grandfathers get the old age pension. But what of the man in between? He pays the taxes for both. Young people have no insoluble problems, and most older folk don't worry a great deal. Why should they? Someone in between youth and maturity does the worrying for them. What is more typical than the summer bachelor who comes home from his office to an empty house and a sink full of dirty dishes in order that his wife and children can enjoy a holiday in the country? What is more typical than the woman who never goes on holidays because her mother is too infirm to travel and cannot be left alone in the house? To middle-age belong the responsibility for children and old people, the paying of bills, the feeling of exhaustion, the nervous breakdowns and coronary attacks. For men, as well as for women, middle-age has its physiological problems. Most suicides occur in middle-age. Between the ages of thirty-five and retirement most of us need the resources of faith more than we have ever needed them before and more than we shall ever need them again.

I am more concerned, however, with the *spiritual* crisis of life's noonday. Reading the twelfth chapter of Ecclesiastes, that familiar passage which begins "Remember now thy Creator in the days of thy youth", have you ever marvelled at its poetic description of old age? "In the day when the keepers of the house (the hands) shall tremble, and the strong men (the legs) shall bow themselves, and the grinders (the teeth) cease because they are few, and those that look out of the windows (the eyes) be darkened." The inevitable break-up at maturity, the destruction at life's eventide. And yet, such destruction need be no more than physical, for as John Quincey Adams said on his eightieth birthday to a friend who inquired after his health, "John Quincey Adams is well. But the house in which he lives at present is becoming dilapidated. It is tottering upon its foundation. Time and the seasons have nearly destroyed it. Its roof is pretty well worn out. Its walls are much shattered and it trembles with every wind. I think John Quincey Adams will have to move out of it soon. But he himself is quite well, quite well." You see—a purely *physical* break-up! The really serious destruction, not of a man's body but of his inner self, can take place long before he becomes eligible for the old age pension. The gravest perils attend us in middle-age.

There is the peril of having reached a dead-end, of having nothing toward which we can look forward. Once Spain stamped on her coins the pillars of Hercules and underneath them the motto "NE PLUS ULTRA", meaning "No More Beyond". That feeling haunts us in middle life, the feeling that so far as life's experiences are concerned we have "had it", and there is no more beyond. Our education lies far behind us. We have launched upon a profession and perhaps gone as far in it as ability and opportunity will allow. No likelihood of further promotions or of further increments in salary. We have married and we have brought our children into the world, as many as we intend to have. Barring sickness and premature death, we shall live in this community and in this house, work at this job, draw this income, and stay married to this wife or husband for the remainder of our days. Life has become fixed, congealed. It promises nothing new, just more of the same thing. The peril of having nothing toward which we can look forward— in a spiritual sense that is "the destruction that wasteth at noonday".

Along with this there sometimes goes a feeling of disillusionment. All our lives we have been looking forward to something, and now that we have arrived, the event is not nearly so exciting as the anticipation. An American college professor tells that as a boy travelling with his parents on a train journey, he stayed up late one night because they were scheduled to cross the Mississippi River at midnight. He had read about that great river in geography and history books, and he felt keenly excited at the prospect of seeing it for the first time; so, despite sleepiness, he kept his eyes open. Finally, as the train rushed across a bridge, he could dimly see a quiet, flat expanse in the starlight. But when his parents said, "There, you've seen the Mississippi," he felt vaguely cheated. It seemed to him that there should have been something more grand than a few glimpses of sluggish water in the darkness. Many people suffer a like disillusionment in the transition from youth to middle-age. They go forward through life's preparatory stages with excited anticipation, confident that they are approaching something magnificent; but passing quickly over the main stream, they suddenly find themselves on the other side. They, too, feel vaguely cheated. They have reached and passed what they were trying to stay awake for, and they say to themselves, "Surely that can't be all there is to it. There ought to be something more." "The destruction that wasteth at noonday."

This leads to a still graver peril, the peril of stagnation. We have to be careful in middle-age lest a scum settle over our spirits, and our ambitions atrophy, and we lose our zest for living, and our lives become dull, prosaic and drab. A modern psychiatrist has labelled this middle-age stagnation, "Chronic circular suburbanitis". In his immortal book *Wind, Sand and Stars*, Antoine de Saint Exupéry, that poetic pioneer in the field of commercial aviation, describes his unuttered feelings toward the typical white-collar employees with whom he used to ride in the bus to the airport:

"Old bureaucrat, my comrade, it is not you who are to blame. No one has ever helped you to escape. You, like a termite, built your peace by blocking up with cement every chink and cranny through which the light might pierce. You rolled yourself up into a ball in your genteel security, in routine, in the stifling conventions of provincial life, raising a modest rampart against the winds and the tides and the stars. You have chosen not to be perturbed by great problems, having trouble enough to forget your own fate as a man. You do not ask yourself questions to which there are no answers. Nobody grasped you by the shoulders while there was still time. Now the clay of which you are shaped has dried and hardened, and naught in you will ever awake the sleeping musician, the poet, the astronomer that possibly inhabited you in the beginning."[1]

Perhaps the most serious peril of middle-age is the peril of a tired cynicism, brought on by a paralysis of ideals. Someone has said that a man is abnormal unless he is a radical at the age of twenty-one and a conservative at the age of thirty-five. Most of us, by the time we reach the half-way mark, have become moral conservatives. In youth we blazed with idealism. We had a sense of individuality. We were different. We could change the world, put colour into our environment, strike the anvil of life like a hammer. Now look at us. Now we have become the anvil, the colourless environment. And such conformists we are, no longer individuals but a type whose personality, clothes, brains and opinions are completely interchangeable with thousands of others of our type. Wordsworth described the process realistically—

> "Heaven lies about us in our infancy!
>   Shades of the prison-house begin to close
>   Upon the growing boy;
>   But he beholds the light, and whence it flows,
>   He sees it in his joy;
>   The Youth, who daily farther from the east
>   Must travel, still is Nature's Priest,

[1] Antoine de Saint Exupéry, *Wind, Sand and Stars* (Harcourt, Brace and World, Inc., New York 1940), p. 23; (Heinemann, London).

> And by the vision splendid
> Is on his way attended;
> At length the Man perceives it die away,
> And fade into the light of common day."

Hopelessness, disillusionment, stagnation, cynicism—these perils beset the man or woman who has reached "the midway of this our mortal life". From a spiritual point of view life's most critical turning-point comes not in youth or in maturity but in middle-age. The crisis, stated simply: How shall life go forward in meaning instead of receding from it? How move toward spiritual freedom instead of settling down into a case of hardening of the spiritual arteries? The powers, skills and ambitions which occupied the centre of attention during our earlier years will no longer suffice. Either fruition must begin to set in or strain and stagnation will most surely set in, and spiritually we shall become people with a promising future behind us. "The destruction that wasteth at noonday."

The Psalmist, however, sings not of life's perils but of the Power protecting him against those perils. See how he begins, "He that dwelleth in the secret place of the Most High shall abide under the shadow of the Almighty." Like all the Hebrew poets, this man, having exhausted his normal vocabulary in praising God's attributes, now turns to the realm of descriptive imagery. Here he conceives of God as a shelter, a fortress—an outdated metaphor in this age of nuclear warfare, but timeless in its truth that when a man sets his life within the context of faith in God, he does secure himself against many of the destructive elements that assault the human soul. How infinitely more true when Christ becomes our Key to the Scriptures, and the Psalmist's God becomes the God of our Christian revelation! It makes a difference in the middle years of a man's life when he believes in the Christian Gospel.

To begin with, the Christian has within him a capacity for renewal which protects him against "the destruction that wasteth at noonday". The greatest thing about believing the Gospel is to know that the entire story of your life has not yet been written, the full development of your personality not yet complete. You need not accept yourself resignedly; you need not rationalize your failings, your weaknesses, your prejudices, by declaring, "Well, that's the way I am. Too late now to do anything about it." Character need never congeal; it can always be renewed. We cannot change the laws of the physical world, the ebb and flow of tides, the forces of gravitation, the stars in their courses; but the lives and habits and purposes of men have been and can be changed. I read a novel in which one of the characters, a small boy, questioned his doctor, "Can you ever get back behind, sir?" "Behind what?" the doctor asked. "And do it again?" said the boy. "Is there any way you can get back behind and do it over again?" "David," replied the doctor, "the greatest thing in the world is to know that God is always beginning again." Paul meant that when he wrote to the Christians at Corinth: "If any man be in Christ, he is a new creature. Old things are passed away; behold all things are become new." We don't have in the Church a bag of tricks that saves life from monotony and stagnation, but we do have in Jesus Christ the only God who can make life worth living for any one of us. We have a God who transforms not the outward circumstances of life, but who does something far more wonderful. He transforms us, makes us different inside, gives us a new mind and hence a new way of looking at life, a new heart, a new motive, a new self. He protects us against "the destruction that wasteth at noonday".

The Christian has another resource which protects him. He has a sense of purpose. It makes all the difference in life to know where you are going. You can sacrifice glamour and put up with a great deal of drudgery, you can accept a monotonous cycle of daily routine and a task that offers little prospect of advancement, provided you can see a meaning in it all, provided you have a sense of purpose. Christ gives us exactly that. The person who believes in Jesus Christ has the same middle-age problems as the next man. He rides in a bus, punches a clock, washes pots and pans, pounds a typewriter and sweeps a floor—but with this difference: a factor outside himself has entered his daily routine and redeemed it from boredom, lifting it into a new context with meaning and purpose. A Canadian Y.W.C.A. secretary who worked among war prisoners in Japan once wrote:

"People often speak to me about what they conceive to be my interesting work. As a matter of fact nothing in all the world can be more prosaic than spending one's life among the unfortunates and failures and the sneaks and thieves and what not, day after day and year after year, unless—unless we believe it is God's chosen work for us to do, and that we cannot escape from it nor it from us. Life, however one views it, is commonplace enough unless one's deepest conviction is that one is a servant of the Most High God, and as such can, to some extent at least, actually enter into the mind of the Master."

These words form the basis of a Christian attitude toward life. If followed and realized, they would save many of us from being destroyed inwardly.

The greatest factor protecting the Christian against "the destruction that wasteth at noonday" is the knowledge that he moves toward a destination. Yes, Spain stamped upon her coins the Pillars of Hercules and beneath them the motto "NE PLUS ULTRA", but Columbus discovered a new world far beyond those pillars, so now the Spanish Government deleted the "NE" and left the "PLUS ULTRA", meaning "More Beyond". Christ has that effect upon our lives. He promises "more beyond", widens our horizon, extends our vision, so that life as it passes the midway mark becomes not dull and deadly, but richer, broader, fuller.

"Grow old along with me!
The best is yet to be,
The last of life, for which the first was made."

Browning was not talking about immortality, at least not in the sense of a geographical destination beyond the grave that becomes our prerogative whether we earn it or not. He was talking of a spiritual destination, a goal which by its very perfection disturbs us, challenges us and beckons us on, a goal which through every stage of our life compels our vision to look onward and upward, and which in the hour of death shines still more dazzlingly because it is of the essence of eternity. "Brethren," wrote the greatest of all Apostles as he lay in prison awaiting death, "I do not consider that I have succeeded; but one thing I do, forgetting what lies behind and straining forward to what lies ahead, I press on toward the goal for the prize of the upward call of God in Christ Jesus." In the commitment of our lives to Christ we are protected against "the destruction that wasteth at noonday".

There is a fable about a boy who devised a scheme whereby to deceive a very wise old man. He would snare a bird, and holding it alive in his hand, would ask, "Is this bird alive or dead?" If the wise man said it was dead, he would open his hand and let the bird fly away. If the wise man said it was alive, the boy would give his hand a quick squeeze, then show the bird dead. Whatever answer he gave the wise man would be wrong. So the boy snared his bird, and holding it in his hand, came with the question, "Mr. Wise Man, is this bird dead or is it alive?" Strangely, the wise man did not look at his hand. Instead he looked full into the boy's eyes and said quietly, "My son, it is whatever you want it to be." So with middle-age, "the midway of this our mortal life." It is whatever we want it to be—spiritual suffocation or spiritual freedom, the soul's death or the soul that through faith in Christ soars upward to God.

9

THE OBLIGATION OF NOBILITY

"Should such a man as I flee?"

(Nehemiah 6:11)

THE HISTORICAL background of this text bears a
striking parallel to the present situation in the Middle
East. For half a century the better classes of the Jews
had been exiled in Babylon. With the fall of Babylon and the
rise of Persia these exiles were emancipated and permitted
to re-establish their homeland in Palestine. Meanwhile,
however, the Arabs had moved in and appropriated their
houses and property, so that when the Jews under Nehemiah
arrived at Jerusalem, there was not exactly a brass band there
to greet them. Ignoring the cool reception, they at once set
to work restoring the destroyed city, a task which, as it
progressed, caused increasing alarm to the surrounding
nations. The Arab leaders came together in emergency
session. A Jewish state threatened their security; it must be
stopped at all costs, and the most obvious point of attack
seemed to be Nehemiah himself. Discredit the leader, and
Jewish morale would collapse.

So they hired a shady little priest named Shemaiah who
secretly approached the Jewish leader with news of a plot
against his life, warning him that unless he took precautions
he would be murdered that very night. And he had a plan
to propose; in fact, he personally would arrange it. Let
Nehemiah take sanctuary in the temple—except, of course,
that Nehemiah, not being a priest, had no right to enter the
temple; to do so would be blasphemy and would certainly
undermine his prestige. It posed a difficult dilemma to the
Jewish statesman, a choice between his principles and his
life. He chose without hesitation. Turning scornfully on

this false informer, he declared, "Should such a man as I flee? And what man such as I am could go into the temple and live? I will not go in."

You can do the whole of this play in modern dress— not only the historical background, but also the characters and the action of the drama. There is nothing more up-to-date than the spectacle of a good man tempted to barter his soul for the sake of safety and security. Not long ago I chatted with a man who resigned from a business firm to take a new position at a considerable decrease in salary. "I had to do it," he explained, "I just couldn't live any longer in that atmosphere of deception and duplicity without becoming a part of it. I am no saint, but I want to do what's right." We all want to do what is right, to maintain what someone has called "the moral grandeur of independent integrity". But integrity comes hard in a world that worships the gods of expediency and compromise, a world that, believing every man to be purchasable, would squeeze him into its crooked mould. Our problem is exactly as Reinhold Niebuhr described it, that of "moral man in an immoral society". In a world that takes evil for granted and accommodates itself to evil, how shall we resist the pressure of evil on our souls?

If fairy stories were true and you could be granted one wish that would make life easier and pleasanter and free from strain, what would it be? For my own part, I think I should ask for a softening of the moral conflict: let the element of temptation be removed from life, let evil lose its allurement, let me be good without having to struggle so hard to be good. Yet I know that such a wish cannot be granted, because it would be a violation of my manhood. God in his wisdom has ordained that human character shall grow and develop through moral struggle; and if we doubt this, let us look at Jesus who came not only to reveal God, but to reveal human life in the length and breadth of its earthly experience. In Christ we see not only that temptation is an integral part of life, but that the higher we ascend in the moral scale, the more insidious and fierce do our temptations become. The nearer we draw to God, the more pronounced our tension with the world's standard of behaviour. What seems perfectly right and acceptable to other people is not right and acceptable to us, and we struggle harder because we struggle alone. We ask again, therefore: in a world that takes evil for granted and accommodates itself to evil, how shall we resist the pressure of evil on our souls?

We can learn something from Nehemiah's manly approach to the problem of evil. Attractively tempted to compromise his highest principles, he turned not to the standards of society or even to the regulations of religion, but rather to the imperatives of his own conscience. He took a good look at himself. "Should such a man as I flee?" It recalls a phrase coined by the French nobility, "*Noblesse Oblige*", meaning that the noble man is under obligation to conduct himself nobly. If we could ponder Nehemiah's experience in the light of the Gospel, if we could search out its motives and implications, we might find it our strongest resource as we, too, fight the battle to maintain the moral grandeur of independent integrity.

I

In the first place, Nehemiah saw himself as a public figure, a man who, in assuming the reins of national leadership, had committed himself to a morally inviolable position. Automatically he must be controlled by a higher standard than that governing other men. Even had he gone into the temple, his conduct would have been less despicable than that of Shemaiah, the wretched little priest-prophet who sold himself as a quisling to the Arabs. But the point was that men of Shemaiah's ilk did things like that. Their moral defections scarcely attracted notice, and people dismissed them with a cynical shrug. Not so Nehemiah. People watched a man in his position, and he knew that having taken a stand on high ground, he must not be deflected from it.

The same principle applies to any public figure—a policeman, a magistrate, a teacher, a politician, a minister of religion. When such men fall they have a long way to

fall, and the world soon takes note of their fall. Newspapers publicize it, gossips gloat over it, and pious people,
who have a savoury collection of skeletons in their own
closets, are quick to throw the first stone. A recent novel
about American politics shows how ruthlessly a man in
public life can be crucified unless he can boast an im-
peccable reputation. It is a shocking commentary on human
cruelty, but perhaps it should be so; perhaps we have a
right to judge by higher standards the man who seeks public
office and presumes to direct the destinies of his fellow-men.

There was a minister who had to resign his parish because he and his wife often quarrelled and finally separated.
The members of his congregation might have played a
reconciling rôle, or at least stood by the poor fellow long
enough to give him a chance to work out his domestic
problems. Instead they promptly resolved themselves into
opposing factions, depending upon whether their sympathies were with the minister or with his wife, and those
who opposed the minister eventually won the day. Not that
these self-appointed judges had any right to cast the first
stone, because some would have fared rather badly in a
public scrutiny of their own moral behaviour. But the
point is that their behaviour is not subject to public scrutiny.
They can commit their indiscretions behind closed doors,
and no one pays any attention to them; but let a leader,
especially a spiritual leader, commit the slightest indiscre-
tion, and he brings upon himself a judgment entirely consistent with his own high status.

This is a word to every Christian. Reading the Gospels,
have you never thought that Jesus dealt over-severely with
the Scribes and Pharisees and other religious leaders of
his day? Certainly it is no wonder that he infuriated them
to a point where it became their consuming passion to get
rid of him. He lashed out at them with such scathing in-
vective, likened them to mausoleums beautifully painted
on the outside but inside full of dead men's bones. He was
forever comparing them unfavourably to publicans and
harlots, the lowest dregs of Jewish society. What they failed
to realize, and what Jesus, with his verbal shock-treatment,

95

tried to impress on them, was that the world expects something of religious people, something it does not expect of those who make no religious profession, and failing to find it, the world quickly shouts "Hypocrite!" in their faces. Peter tells us that as Christians we have been "born to the purple"; we are "a chosen generation, a royal priesthood". But, he adds, "the time has come for judgment to begin with the house of God." We who belong to the Church have identified ourselves with the spiritual nobility, and to call ourselves noble carries with it the obligation to conduct ourselves nobly.

II

We can say further that Nehemiah was deeply conscious of the trust which had been committed to him. Back in Babylon he had so gained the King's confidence as to be appointed cupbearer in the Royal Household. Indeed, the King released the Jewish exiles only because Nehemiah pleaded for it and because he promised to lead the expedition back to Jerusalem and personally supervise the rebuilding of the city. As a man greatly trusted, he knew that it would be an outright betrayal of that trust to follow any course of action, however expedient, that might weaken his leadership and jeopardize the national safety. Enter the temple? It would be unthinkable! "Should such a man as I flee?"

Before compromising his highest principles a man had better ponder the repercussions on those who love and trust him. Arthur Miller dramatized that truth in his powerful play, *Death of a Salesman*. Loud-mouthed Willie Loman loved his two sons, but he never realized that in blowing himself up to such a colossal size he had fashioned a sacred idol in their imagination. The boys worshipped him, hung on his every word, believed that he could do no wrong. They accepted his smooth talk about tricky deals and clever deceptions as the normal ways of business that any smart man must practise in order to get ahead. It never occurred to them to question their father's mediocrity, or the growing prosperity of the honest neighbours next door, or their own failure and unpopularity at school. Then one day the elder son discovered that his idol had feet of clay. Expelled from school, the boy hopped on a bus and travelled to the city where his father was doing business, expecting to receive there the usual sympathy, the usual self-justification. But bursting into his father's hotel room, he found the older man slightly drunk and in the act of presenting a pair of silk stockings to a brazen, half-dressed young woman. Realizing the awful truth, the lad fell to the floor sobbing, and from the climactic moment the tragedy gathered momentum as it moved toward estrangement, despair and finally suicide.

"I would be true, for there are those who trust me;
I would be pure, for there are those who care;
I would be strong, for there is much to suffer;
I would be brave, for there is much to dare."

Does a man feel the urge towards what he knows to be low and mean and ugly? Then let him remember what he represents to those who love and trust him, the blind confidence which they place in him, the agony they will suffer and the possible consequences to their lives if he lets them down. Let him think of his parents who cherished to the grave the vision of an eager, idealistic youth marching into life's battle with the moral purity of a crusader. Let him think of his wife whose happiness he holds in his hands and whose heart will break if he crushes that happiness like a helpless and delicate flower. Let him think of his children who cling to him as to a rock and who would follow him into hell if he gave the word. We have all been given a portion of human love and trust in larger measure than we can deserve or understand, and simply to be conscious of it and to thank God for it is to find it a tremendous resource of moral strength.

III

Then Nehemiah would have regard to the possible influence of his behaviour. He would reckon with its effect on his people. If he committed this blasphemy against God, he would be discredited, of course, washed-up as a leader; a worthier man would have to replace him. But it was not as simple as all that. Of the profligate priest Chaucer wrote, "If gold rust, what shall iron do?" To the Jewish people Nehemiah represented gold, something infinitely precious and durable. As long as he remained faithful, they could remain faithful; his strength became their strength, his hope their hope. In a sense he personified all that they were working for, and there could be no doubt that with his collapse the morale of his people would collapse and the rebuilding of Jerusalem end in failure. His enemies knew that, and he knew it, and that is why he retorted contemptuously, "Should such a man as I flee?"

You often hear a person excuse some moral licence by exclaiming, "It's my own business! I have no one to hurt but myself!" How tragically untrue! No man can fall without dragging others down with him. Each one of us exercises an unconscious character influence on the people who surround us every day. The things we do, the attitudes we take, the words we speak fall like stones into a pond sending out endless ripples of unbelievable influence. If there is a Christian argument for total abstinence from strong drink, it is not to be found in the mythologies of old-fashioned temperance societies, but rather in the gospel of love as reasonably presented by the Apostle Paul. It seems that in the early Church some Christians felt a compulsion to abstain from certain types of food and drink. Others, of stronger character, tended to ridicule this puritanical abstemiousness, deeming it superfluous to Christian experience and service. Paul enjoined abstinence, not for one's own sake —though an impressive argument could be offered on that very point—but for the sake of its strengthening influence on the weaker brethren. He said, "It is good neither to eat flesh, nor to drink wine, nor anything whereby thy brother stumbleth, or is offended, or is made weak."

I am sure that if once we realized our influence potential, we should want to be straight and upright and incorruptible and self-disciplined. We should know that our moral decisions can never be a private affair, that unconsciously others are taking their cue from us and that by the strength of our influence they stand or fall. O'Henry, that supreme master of the short story, has a tale about a country boy who migrated to a large city and there learned to walk the wrong way. He became a pickpocket, a successful pickpocket. One day, pleased with himself after he had stolen a fat wallet, he noticed a sweet, gentle girl of his own age; he looked again and he recognized her. She had sat beside him in the same class in the village school in the days when he had been young and good and innocent. She did not see him, but the very sight of her made him catch a glimpse of himself. He suddenly saw himself for the petty sneak-thief that he was. He leaned his burning forehead against the cool iron of a lamp post. "God," he said, "how I hate myself!" In spite of what he was and of what he had done, he was still vulnerable to the silent influence of goodness. Such influence you and I can exercise every day, and to exercise it is the obligation of nobility.

IV

Certainly Nehemiah's decision must have been a religious decision. Beyond all considerations of position, trust and influence, lay the immensely important fact that he saw himself as a servant of the Most High God. The Jews were God's people, Canaan the land of God's promise, the Persian King God's instrument of liberation, and the rebuilding of Jerusalem God's purpose. Nehemiah would know himself called of God to the task of rebuilding the Holy City and restoring its sacred sanctuary. On his conscience rested the burden of Divine imperative—which meant that defection would be more than moral failure; it would be disobedience toward God and therefore sin. Here was the secret of Nehemiah's strength, the resource that stiffened his moral backbone and enabled him to retort, "Should such a man as I flee?"

The editor of a great newspaper published this prayer for a newly inaugurated President of the United States, "O

Lord, give him the courage, not of his convictions, but of your commandments." No man will ever stand really firm in the presence of evil until he sees himself as a servant of God, and therefore sees evil for what it really is—the disobedience of God's law and the betrayal of his love. Is that not, after all, the whole basis of morality in our Western world? Why do we object to the publication of obscene literature? Why do we revolt against sexual promiscuity, drunkenness, dope addiction, swindling, embezzlement and murder? Because these things are not socially acceptable? On the contrary, they may be very acceptable in some anti-God political régime that reverses the labels, calling black white and white black. Or is it that they do damage to our personalities? On the contrary, there is a school of thought which believes that the greatest damage lies in repression and self-discipline. No, our society revolts against the great moral and social evils because these things are wrong, everlastingly wrong, and because to do them is to violate the moral laws which from the beginning of time have been written into the constitution of the universe, laws which cannot be violated with impunity.

"Mother," a child asked, "what makes your hands so scarred and twisted?" "My child," replied the mother, "when you were a baby I was awakened one night by the smell of smoke. The house was on fire. I thought immediately of you, and rushing to your room I found the flames surrounding your bed. I beat at them with my hands, picked you up and carried you to safety. In doing this, I burned my hands, and they have been scarred and twisted ever since." On the great heart of God is a scar which, when all other considerations have been swept aside, remains our supreme resource of moral strength. We resist evil, not for fear of breaking God's laws, but for love of God, because God has declared his love for us in the death of his Son on Calvary's Cross. I see him there, lonely, mocked, beaten, spat upon, his lifeblood slowly ebbing away, his body racked with pain, his features twisted in agonizing grief, and I ask myself, "Am I really worth that to God—that to save me he should burn himself in the fires of human wickedness? Does he go that far to constrain the love and obedience of my poor, worthless heart?" Here surely is the highest ground of my nobility— that I am a man for whom Christ died. "Should such a man as I flee?"

IO

THE MAIN BUSINESS OF LIVING

"But seek first his Kingdom and his righteousness, and all
these things shall be yours as well."

(St. Matthew 6:33)

J. S. BONNELL BEGINS a chapter in his book, *No Escape
from Life*, by recalling an incident that happened in New
York on July 26, 1938. On an eighteen-inch ledge
seventeen stories above the street on the front of the Gotham
Hotel a young man stood for eleven hours in agonizing
suspense. Down in the streets a morbid crowd of ten thousand
also waited—waited to see him jump as he had calmly
announced his intention of doing. One by one, relatives and
sympathetic people went to the window and pleaded with
the youth—his sister, friends, firemen, policemen, psychologists, a priest from St. Patrick's Cathedral, the Deputy
Mayor of New York, and others. Quietly but adamantly
he refused to enter the window. "I wish someone would
convince me that life is worth living," he said. Just as pre-
parations were concluded for two men to be lowered from
the floor above and a cargo net to be lifted from below, he
leaped to his death.[1]

Suicide is taking place across North America at the rate
of sixty deaths a day; attempted suicide, according to
current estimates, occurs every four minutes. In Britain there
were some five thousand suicides in 1960. A study of world-
wide statistics reveals that one-quarter million people take
their own lives every year, and that three times that number
attempt it without success. On top of that we have no way
of computing the "hidden suicides", the multitudes who

[1] Harper and Brothers, Publishers (New York 1958), pp. 104–105

harbour within themselves that impulse to self-destruction which psychologists call "the unconscious death wish". One medical expert has said: "Chronic illness and disability, neurosis in its manifold forms, drug and alcohol addiction, 'martyrdom', life patterns of repetitious failure, accident proneness, are all to variable degrees motivated by the tendency of the human being to turn his aggressive drives upon himself, to act in more or less overt ways as his own executioner."

What brings an intelligent person to the point where he can find no answer to the problem of life except to take the final route of escape from it? These have been given as the usual reasons: an unhappy love affair, emotional maladjustment, chronic illness, economic problems, revenge, imitation, effort to avoid disgrace or to save others from trouble and distress. Psychologists have long since learned that in any one case of suicide the complex causes go far deeper than the superficial reasons given to the newspapers. One thing certain: there are many tragic figures like the young man in New York who resign from the human race because they can see no further reason for belonging to it. Life has not been unkind to them. They cannot plead ill-health or financial difficulty or loneliness. They have plenty to live *with*, but the trouble is that they have nothing to live *for*, no sense of meaning or purpose that makes it worthwhile for them to continue breathing. Futility paralyses their souls. Life has become for them a ghastly and answerless riddle, "a tale told by an idiot, full of sound and fury, signifying nothing." Nobody has yet convinced them that life is worth living.

Gerald Kennedy recounts the rather startling experience of a man who visited the Bell Laboratories. On the desk of one of the executives he saw a machine that truly represents the end of the line. It was a small wooden casket the size of a cigar box with a single switch on the side. When you flip the switch there is a buzzing sound, and the lid slowly rises so that a hand can emerge. The hand reaches down, turns off the switch and goes back into the box. The lid then comes down and the buzzing ceases. That's all there is to it—a machine that does nothing but switch itself off.[1] It might be funny except that it symbolizes a great many human lives, people who waken each morning for no other purpose than to fall asleep again each evening; not stupid people—they might be happier if they were; not bad people—evil might bring them into closer touch with reality; just human machines going through the same meaningless motions day after day, and because of it, driven to various forms of escape.

What a dramatic difference in people when they discover a purpose for living. After the war a motion picture enjoyed great popularity and won several academy awards for its grasp of the problem faced by our fighting men in their repatriation to civilian life. Its saddest feature was the accuracy of the title, *The Best Years of Our Lives*. For some people the war years were the best of their lives, just because they had something to live for then, a purpose of tremendous significance that absorbed them, consumed them and made them forget their own little neuroses.

Life, to be worth living, must have a purpose, a larger purpose than its own preservation and comfort. Food, clothing, shelter—these things are important, especially when you do not possess them, as the starving and homeless refugees in Europe and Asia would quickly testify. We all have to go through the motions of earning a living and providing ourselves and our families with the basic necessities. If we make these things *the main business of life*, however, we insult our personalities; we treat ourselves as something less than human beings. Jesus meant that when he said to the disciples, "Is not the life more than food and the body more than clothing?" We require food and clothing and shelter in order to survive, but we cannot devote our God-given capacities simply to the provision of bigger and better survival kits, any more than soldiers can win a war by lounging about the kitchen and filling their sacks with rations. Life must have a larger purpose than the pampering of our bodies and the accumulation of grown-up toys, else it is not life at all.

Even a wrong purpose can redeem life from futility. At

[1] Gerald Kennedy, *The Parables* (Harper and Brothers, Publishers, New York 1960), p. 38

the close of the war a Russian soldier said to an American soldier in Berlin, "We Communists are happy, not because we are rich, but because we know where we are going." Let us be crystal clear about one thing. When we face the fact of the Communist world today, we are facing not only a totalitarian political system, not only a socialist economic system, not only a highly-geared educational system, not only a vast military machine. Behind and under and all around these things is a faith, a religious faith without God— the faith that the universe is built in such a way and history determined in such a way, that the goals of Communism will ultimately triumph. Nothing could be more naïve than the assumption that we shall shake the faith of the Communist by pointing out to him that Western plumbing is better, that we drive more motor-cars per capita, that our women wear more attractive clothes. We only amuse if not insult the Communist by throwing these things in his face. He has a larger purpose than gratifying his own physical appetites, and that sense of purpose gives meaning to his life.

It is difficult to find any such sense of purpose in our Western society today. Except for a few visionaries, a few dedicated statesmen and journalists and artists and prophets, we do not as a people give the world the impression that we know where we are going. We have goals, to be sure, but such limited goals. Our characteristic words are "preserve" and "defend". We must preserve our way of life; we must defend our freedom. We give the impression of a people who have "arrived", who have created a comfortable nest for ourselves in our snug corner of this windswept planet and whose main business is to stay there and secure ourselves against every storm. When issues do disturb our complacency, they are not the great world issues, but the selfish, material, domestic problems that concern our happiness and privilege and standard of living—the symptoms of moral paralysis. C. S. Lewis pictures the devil instructing his minions: "Above all, get this earthly creature, man, thinking of himself, of what happens to him instead of what he ought to be doing. Take all sense of purpose and dedication out of his life and he will become the obedient servant of hell."[1]

We find this gem buried in the sermons of Phillips Brooks:

"Bad will be the day for every man when he becomes so absolutely contented with the life that he is living, with the thoughts that he is thinking, with the deeds that he is doing, when there is not forever beating at the doors of his soul some great desire to do something larger, which he knows that he was meant and made to do because he is still, in spite of all, the child of God."

If life for any one of us is going to be meaningful, then very early we have to decide what shall be *the main business of living*. We have to ask the question, Where am I going? What am I living for? To what purpose can I dedicate my highest energies regardless of what happens to me, regardless of riches or poverty, sickness or health? The late Thomas Dooley was a young American doctor who resigned his commission in the navy to serve the suffering people in Indo-China. Soon afterwards he fell sick with a malignant tumour in his chest and was flown back to the United States for treatment. As a doctor he estimated that he might have five or six years to live with this "capricious type of cancer". As a missionary, he decided to return to Laos and give these remaining years to his new calling. You see the contrast. One young man leaps from a hotel window because no one has convinced him that life is worth living; another clings jealously to these earthly surroundings because life for him has worthier goals than his own health and happiness.

The supreme contribution of vital Christianity to a man's life is that it invests that life with a larger purpose than his own comfort and security. I say *vital* Christianity, because nothing comes of a mere "interest" in religion or a mere conventional Church relationship. Any minister who has ever read the burial service can tell you that Church affiliation is no deterrent to suicide. Something happens, however, when a person goes beneath the level of respectable piety to a deep, genuine, first-hand saving experience of God in

[1] C. S. Lewis, *The Screwtape Letters* (Geoffrey Bles, London 1942), p. 34

Jesus Christ. Something happens to the man who by an act of faith becomes a man in Christ, so that the heart of Christ beats in his bosom and the mind of Christ thinks in his brain, and he can say with Paul, "I am crucified with Christ; it is no longer I who live, but Christ liveth in me." To that man Christ gives an all-consuming purpose, the very purpose that motivated his own life upon earth, the shining goal toward which he moved, about which he preached, for which he strove and lived and died and which in his own person he incarnated. He calls it "the Kingdom of God". "This Kingdom," he says, "is the highest good in life, like a treasure hidden in a field or a pearl of great price. When you find it, you will make any sacrifice to possess it. Earthly things will seem valueless alongside its surpassing worth and beauty. . . . Let this be your purpose, let this be your goal, let this be the main business of your life. . . . Seek first the Kingdom of God and his righteousness, and these other things, food and clothing and shelter, shall, in the providence of God, be yours as well, according as you need them."

We must not be vague here. We must not allow this transcendent truth to remain trapped in Biblical thought-forms. We are dealing with a vital matter, something that touches the most sensitive spot in our complex personalities. This is no academic question but an issue of burning and crucial importance: What gives meaning to life? What goal, what purpose can so absorb us in the totality of our being that life is shot through with meaning and radiance and becomes pre-eminently worth living? The Christian answer comes back, "Seek ye first the Kingdom of God," but what is the Kingdom of God? We can define it theologically as the reign of God, his Sovereignty over all life in this age and his righteous rule in the age to come. What does it mean, however, as a personal, present, practical reality, a goal which the individual can seek and enter and possess here and now? What does it mean to a young man who teeters on a window-ledge a hundred and sixty feet above the pavement and says, "I wish someone would convince me that life is worth living"?

We can say that a man begins his search for the Kingdom

by choosing a vocation that allows opportunities of usefulness and service. To be sure, all of us cannot work directly
with people; many must work with machines and merchandise a long way removed from the product of their labours.
Too many young men and women, however, exclude the
dimension of service from their thinking even when they
plan their life's work. A Canadian Broadcasting Corporation
reporter interviewed some of the seventy thousand students
in Canadian universities, asking them the question, "Why
did you go to college?" Almost without exception they confessed the economic motive. A higher education would equip
them for better jobs, increase their earning power, put more
money into their pockets, guarantee them security. They
may not know it, but some have already begun their climb
to a seventeenth-storey window-ledge, because in college
terminology they are "majoring on minors", on goals that
are simply not big enough for their God-given intelligence.
There was a pastor who rejoiced recently when two different
people in his congregation told him that they were taking
new positions at a considerable sacrifice in salary, but doing
so because the positions afforded greater opportunities of
working with people and helping them. Perhaps neither
acted from a direct religious motive, but both were unconsciously seeking the Kingdom of God.

A man's decisions will be shaped by the sense of purpose
running through his life. If he seeks the Kingdom of God,
he will be a man under obedience to God, a man who in
every situation tries to learn the will of God and act according
to it. He will be a man of prayer who works things out on
his knees, like Abraham Lincoln praying through half the
night to determine his stand on the slavery issue when the
entire government threatened to oppose him for it. A man
who seeks God's Kingdom will ask one question, not "What
do I want?" but, "Lord, what wilt thou have me to do?"
That one question will touch all the decisions of his daily life
—how he votes at a board meeting, his support of political
candidates, the budgeting of his income, the use of his leisure,
the upbringing of his children, the choice of his friends.
There is nothing to describe the exhilaration that floods your

soul when once you have clearly discerned the will of God in a situation and given it priority over your own will; in that moment you feel yourself very close to the Kingdom of God.

The Kingdom-seeker will make his life a centre of Christian influence, and he will do this without any regard to the circumstances in which he lives. The Quakers have a motto: "It is better to light a candle than to curse the darkness." The Christian does exactly that. In the darkness of duplicity he lights a candle of honour; in the darkness of prejudice he lights a candle of tolerance; in the darkness of luxury he lights a candle of modesty; in the darkness of suffering he lights a candle of courage. Henry Jones is not an important man by ordinary standards. He works in a government office from nine to five, draws a moderate income, and rarely does anything more exciting than spray the roses in his garden. But hell's foundations tremble when Henry Jones walks into the office, because while people consider him a bit stuffy, they respect him; they never gossip and they never talk profanely in his presence. If there is anywhere on earth such a thing as the Kingdom of God in microcosm, you will find it in Henry Jones' home, in the love and affection and mutual trust of husband and wife and of parents and children. Henry Jones may not be an important man; in terms of money and success he may not have very much to live *with*; but he has plenty to live *for*—and you can catch a glimpse of it when he and his family kneel for prayers each evening after dinner—a purpose that transfigures his life with meaning.

Whoever seeks the Kingdom of God will want to have a share in some corporate Christian witness. Have you ever known a really active and faithful Church member who was an alcoholic? There are alcoholics in every congregation, chronic drinkers; they keep a bottle at home and at the office; they drink alone, they drink to escape boredom, they drink to fill that yawning emptiness at the centre of their souls. You may argue that any worthwhile avocation, politics, culture, sport, community service, a hobby, will so give significance to a man's life that he need not turn to spurious substitutes. But do they give significance? Let your own experience decide. Is it not true that people who love the Church, its worship, its fellowship, its witness and its mission are the people who in your experience live lives that are radiant with meaning and purpose? Why? Because they have a sense of going somewhere, of moving toward goals that are not limited goals. They seek the Kingdom of God.

In his recent biography of Albert Schweitzer, Norman Cousins tries to convey the impression of a man who has learned to use himself fully.[1] He says that much of the ache and brooding unhappiness in modern life is the result of man's inability to use himself fully. Rarely do we realize our God-given potential; rarely do we release the yearnings and the powers of our personalities; rarely do we have a sense of fulfilling ourselves through total contact with total challenge. Therefore happiness eludes us. But Schweitzer, says Norman Cousins, is a man less concerned with happiness than with purpose. One supreme goal beckons him on and inspires his heroic missionary labours. He calls that goal by its Biblical name, the Kingdom of God. He has written a book entitled *The Kingdom of God*, as yet unpublished, and when Cousins asked to see the manuscript, the conversation went like this: "Where is *The Kingdom of God* now?" "Right here at the hospital," replied Schweitzer. The great doctor had spoken a larger truth than he realized at the moment. He had disclosed the secret of his own life; for there in the jungle hospital at Lambaréné, a place without any of the comforts, the conveniences, the luxuries that we break our necks to possess, is an order of obedience to God and service to man which has produced the most significant human life of our century.

[1] Norman Cousins, *Dr. Schweitzer of Lambaréné* (Harper and Brothers, Publishers, New York 1960)

II

THE MAN OUTSIDE THE CHURCH

"When Jesus heard this he marvelled at him, and turned
and said to the multitude that followed him, 'I tell you, not
even in Israel have I found such faith.' "

(St. Luke 7:9)

I HAVE ALWAYS admired this Roman Centurion of whom
Jesus spoke. He differs so remarkably from the normal run
of centurions, those officers of ancient Rome who commanded military garrisons in occupied countries. We have
a fairly clear picture of what most of them were like—arrogant, coarse, sometimes brutal, as witnessed by their callous cruelty on the day of our Lord's crucifixion. But here
was a different type altogether—refined, sensitive, humane;
one to whom a subject people were still people and not
cattle. This man respected the Jews and he coveted their
respect instead of their fear.

Whether attracted to the Jewish religious faith or not, he
could still see the value of supporting that faith instead of
ridiculing it; he had even done the generous thing of providing funds for the building of a new synagogue. And now
he wanted Jesus to heal his sick servant. It bespoke an
unusual regard for human personality that a Roman centurion should display such affectionate concern for a slave
whom, after all, society valued no higher than a piece of real
estate. The reticence of his approach to Jesus—sending first
the elders of the synagogue, then friends, as though to acknowledge his unworthiness to enter the Master's presence—
suggests in this pagan military officer a reverence and a
humility that the Master rarely found even in professedly
religious people. Still more remarkable was his spiritual
discernment and his instinctive recognition, as a soldier,

of the Divine authority that was in Jesus. This Roman centurion saw what many devout Jews failed to see, namely,
that Jesus of Nazareth could, if he wanted, heal the sick slave.
Do you wonder that Jesus so readily acceded to his request,
marvelling and rejoicing at the dignity and simplicity of
this man's faith? "I tell you," he said to the multitude that
followed him, "I tell you that not even in Israel have I
found such faith."

There is something familiar about this Roman Centurion.
He typifies the man outside the Church, the man who, while
professing no allegiance to the community of religious faith,
yet displays to a remarkable degree the essential spirit of
religious faith. I think we are willing to admit that not all
religious people are inside the Church. Most of them are,
of course, but every now and then you encounter some
admirable, unselfish, but quite unchurched individual who
seems like a walking argument against organized religion.
Mrs. Smith (and I have purposely altered her name) is one
of the most enthusiastically orthodox Christians whom I
know. Some would call her "fundamentalist". She is the
type who backs you into a corner and shoves her face up
against yours, and says, "You have not been saved yet!
You have not given your life to Jesus!" Mrs. Smith chases
souls for Jesus like a lepidopterist chasing butterflies—all
except one soul. She goes to a Jewish dressmaker, an honourable, devout, God-fearing man, but, of course, not a Christian, and altogether unimpressed by Mrs. Smith. How does
she explain him to her friends? She tells them that he is a
"secret Christian", which means that he is a Christian without
knowing that he is a Christian. Mrs. Smith is really trying
to get around her intractably fundamentalist position and
come to terms with the fact that not all religious people are
inside the Church.

The Bible itself does not pretend that the Church has a
monopoly on religion. The Bible talks about the sovereignty
of God, and that means that God does not stand idly
around shifting from one foot to the other, waiting to be
recognized or received before he can do something with
human life. God in Christ is the Lord of all life and the

source of all good, no matter what name it uses or where it is found. Within the Church these days we deplore the secularism which has penetrated all areas of our culture as a worm penetrates the fruit on a tree. "Where," we inquire sadly, "are the religious themes that dominated the art, the music, the literature of two centuries ago?" Once men built their universities, painted their pictures and composed their symphonies to the glory of God; now they glorify themselves, and the chaos of their efforts reflects it. Does that mean, however, that we can write off modern culture as irreligious? The truth we have to consider is that all those areas of life which we commonly denote as secular, far from being devoid of religion, may come closer to the heart of true spirituality than we have readily imagined. This becomes evident when we mark out the elements which go into the making of a religious life.

The supreme characteristic of a religious life is a fundamental *sense of reverence*. Call it by many names—humility, wonder, mysticism. Rudolph Otto gives a classic definition in what he terms "The Idea of the Holy". The raw material of religion he finds in the sense of the "numinous", a shuddering awe before the tremendous and fascinating mystery which meets a man in the midst of his experience of the world. An old prayer of the Breton fishermen brings it within our understanding. As they cast off from the shores of France to face the sweep and toss and swell of deep waters, they looked up to heaven and said, "O God, thy sea is so great and my boat is so small." Just that. No more than that. And that is where true religion begins—with a man pausing to stand consciously before a universe that overwhelms him, a universe at the heart of which is mystery, something greater than himself, something older and more powerful and more wonderful.

This sense of reverence in the presence of ultimate mystery, while you find it at the heart of all Biblical religion, is by no means the monopoly of orthodox Christianity. Indeed, the Church may become so humanistic in its worship and so secular in its outlook as to lose the dimension of the supernatural altogether. It is a strange thing to say, but this most essential element in religion sometimes appears more evident in a scientific laboratory than in a church. The late Albert Einstein was not a practising Jew; he belonged to no orthodox religious community, yet Einstein called himself a religious man, and he had a right to do so. Listen to his own words:

> "The most beautiful thing we can experience is the mysterious. It is the source of all true art and science. He to whom this emotion is a stranger, who can no longer pause to wonder and stand rapt in awe, is as good as dead; his eyes are closed. This insight into the mystery of life, coupled though it be with fear, has given rise to religion. To know that what is impenetrable to us really exists, manifesting itself as the highest wisdom and the most radiant beauty which our dull faculties can comprehend only in their most primitive forms—this knowledge, this feeling is at the centre of true religiousness. In this sense, and in this sense only, I belong to the ranks of devoutly religious men."

Another element in the religious life is its *concern with Reality*, and where Christianity exists in loyalty to the Word of God, it forces men to reckon with life's profound realities. A prominent clergyman tells how he walked the streets of an American city one night with a man terribly disturbed because he could not believe in God. This was a man of deep human sympathies, great ability and wide achievement for good, who longed to accept the Faith but could not. The minister thought of the members of his own congregation, many of whom did believe in God because they had been brought up to believe and had never faced tears and misery sympathetically enough to have their faith shaken. He compared them with this doubter, this fine-grained doubter who, because of his very love for people, his sense of justice, his resentment at the "sufferings that fell with such terrific incidence upon the vast, obscure, forgotten masses of mankind", kept turning at every stoplight to ask, "How can you believe that a good God made a world like this?"[1]

Again, it is a strange thing to say, but if the essence of religion lies in a concern with Reality, then there may be as

[1] As told by Frederick B. Speakman in *Love is Something You Do* (Fleming H. Revell Co., Westwood, New Jersey 1959), p. 83

much religion outside the Church as in it. There was a profoundly provoking book published in America three years ago entitled *The Beat Generation and the Angry Young Men*,[1] an anthology edited by two agnostic Jews and claiming to "represent many of the most brilliant and significant writers of our times". Pimps, junkies, pool-sharks, geeks, fixters, hipsters—these are the colourful characters one meets in four hundred pages of concentrated neurosis and nausea. I can only quote my own comment appended to one of the selections. I wrote, "This man makes me want to vomit. He crawls the gutter of ingratitude, cynicism and cheap melodrama. Why universalize abnormality and call it representative?" Yet something about the book haunted me, and I reluctantly agreed with the editors that "the basic impulse of the Beat Generation is a religious one". If by religion we mean a concern with Reality, life's deepest issues, its origin, its meaning, its purpose, its destiny, then such a volume, however revolting, cannot be lightly dismissed. The Angry Young Men refuse to face religious answers, but at least they are asking religious questions. Their concern is with the human soul in its relation to the universe, a concern sometimes more acute outside the Church than in it.

Then, the religious life is marked by its *high ethical* sense. The great prophets of Israel brought to their people the penetrating insight that because God is a moral God, therefore our relationship with him must be a moral relationship; by itself any other relationship is an hypocrisy and an abomination. "He hath showed thee, O man, what is good; and what doth the Lord require of thee but to do justly and to love mercy and to walk humbly with thy God?" "You have faith and I have works," writes the Apostle James, "show me your faith apart from your works, and I by my works will show you my faith." The moral Leader of mankind concluded his greatest ethical teaching by saying that the difference between a religion that embodies this teaching and one that fails to embody it is precisely the difference between a house built on rock and a house built on sand.

[1] Ed. Gene Feldman and Max Gartenberg (The Citadel Press, New York 1958)

One thing never ceases to disturb me. If religion be defined as social and moral responsibility, then the soil in which it flourishes may sometimes be found more plenteously outside the Church than in it. It sobers one to realize how many of the great humanitarians, the social reformers and public servants have lived and worked independently of organized Christianity. I have read two biographies of Sir William Osler, totalling some eighteen hundred pages in all, and nowhere do I find in the words of the writers or in Osler's own words a single acknowledgment of indebtedness to the Church. Yet Osler was a profoundly religious man both in his philosophy of life and more especially in his large, sympathetic and kindly spirit. One biographer describes him walking down the main street of Montreal on a bitterly cold winter morning and taking off his overcoat and putting it on the back of a starving beggar. That typified the young man who later became Regius Professor of Medicine at Oxford and drew from more than one of his friends a comment like this : "My intimate associations with him as guide, philosopher and friend from earliest years until his death lead me to the belief that he was of all men the most Christ-like in his life and the most God-like in his attitudes." The biographer concludes the Montreal incident by saying, "It is singular how all who were thrown with Dr. Osler felt his likeness to Christ. Always before them they saw the Divine Physician. They could not see the one without thinking of the other."[1] But still no reference to the Church.

Above all, the religious life is a dedicated life, its crowning characteristic an *unqualified commitment* to some supreme object of devotion. In this supreme object of devotion the religious man finds his salvation and to it he gives his ultimate loyalty. It becomes his god. He worships it, prostrates himself before its altar, and will make any sacrifice for it, because in it he finds the meaning of life. If a man *has* such an object of devotion—be it money, work, home, public service, dialectical materialism, or the God and Father of our Lord Jesus Christ—if there is something outside himself

[1] Edith Gittings Reid, *The Great Physician* (Oxford University Press, New York 1931), pp. 55–56

to which he is completely dedicated, then that man is a religious man.

Not for a moment shall we pretend that the sense of high dedication exists only within the bounds of organized Christianity. L. P. Jacks said of a friend, "Look at him; isn't he an inspiration? He spends his breath arguing that there is no God, but spends his life proving that there is." You all know people like that, godless in their conversation, yet so godlike in their high devotion. You meet them in all walks of life: the scientist who, while he seems to maintain an attitude of agnosticism, makes his laboratory a shrine of unselfish dedication; the physician who, while too busy to be in God's House on Sunday morning, cares for his patients with the tender concern of One who himself healed the sick; the statesman who makes no public appearances at Church worship, but who fearlessly champions the cause of social justice and truly serves those who have elected him; the teacher who never mentions the name of God, yet who, beyond informing human minds, gives herself lovingly and devotedly to the moulding of Christian character; the parent who, while seemingly indifferent to the religious education of her children, yet creates in her home an atmosphere of high religious ideals. It is said that when someone asked Sir Winston Churchill if he supported the Church, he replied, "Yes, but not as a pillar on the inside; rather as a buttress that holds it up from the outside."

"When Jesus heard this he marvelled at him, and turned and said to the multitude that followed him, 'I tell you, not even in Israel have I found such faith'." Reverence, concern with Reality, a moral sense, high dedication—all of these elements that go into the making of a religious life can be found outside the bounds of organized Christianity. Wherever you go, you meet him and you respect him, the modern counterpart of the Roman Centurion, the man outside the Church.

He *judges* us, this man outside the Church; he brings into bold relief the paltriness of our Christianity and compels us to ask ourselves, "What do ye more than others?" We have always considered these qualities—reverence, realism, morality and dedication—to be the distinctively Christian virtues that belong peculiarly to people within the House- hold of Faith; but here is a man outside the Household of Faith who possesses all of them to a degree that puts us to shame. It can only mean one of two things; either we have been wasting our time in the faith and practice of Chris- tianity, or else we have never gone deeper than a superficial application of Christianity to our lives. Many of these people outside the Church are not antagonistic to the Church. They are waiting to be convinced; but looking at us, they can simply see no reason for belonging to the Church. They have all that we possess and more besides.

That saintly man, Mahatma Gandhi, who exercised such powerful influence over India's three hundred and fifty million people, was not far from the Kingdom of God; modern Christianity has produced few spiritual giants to compare with him. Gandhi was so profoundly affected by the teachings of Jesus that at one point in his early life he nearly became a Christian. He told of his contact with a Christian family in South Africa who gave him a standing invitation to dinner every Sunday and afterward took him to the Wesleyan Church. The service, apparently, did not make a favourable impression on young Gandhi. He found the sermons uninspiring. In fact, the congregation did not strike him as being particularly religious at all. They were not an assembly of devout souls that would appeal to this innately mystical young man, but rather an aggregation of worldly minded people going to church merely as a sign of social and cultural respectability. Gandhi confessed that he had a hard time keeping awake and would have felt ashamed except that some of his white-skinned neighbours suffered the same difficulty. He said, "I could not go on long like this and soon gave up attending the service."

He *inspires* us, this man outside the Church. We do him an injustice if we allow him merely to embarrass us and drive us into the misery of self-reproach. He makes no invidious comparisons. He does not go around preening himself on his superiority and saying, "See how much better I am than those Church folk." To be sure, some people do adopt that priggish pose, and they have their reward, but we are not talking about them. We are talking about the people whom we know and respect for their high level of moral and spiritual excellence and who seem to have attained this level without the impulses and resources of conventional Christianity. They would be the last to derive a morbid satisfaction from their superiority over professed Christians and the first to recognize and respect a higher level of excellence when they see it. They do not condemn us; they inspire us; they become our greatest incentive to holier and Christlike living.

Look at it this way. Suppose after many years of study you graduate from a school of architecture, fully qualified, capable of designing a structure according to any specification. Starting out in business, you find yourself competing with another school, the "Do-it-Yourself" School. A man says to you, "I don't need an architect. I can design a house and build most of it myself." "Preposterous!" you retort. "No one can build a house unless he does it according to the rules. Let me see some of these home-made efforts." And having said that, do you look at the quonsit huts and clapboard shacks that will soon become a slum? No, you inspect the most modern and solidly built bungalow and make that your standard of reference. That is what you must surpass in order to justify your formal training in architecture. So in the Christian life, we do not compare ourselves with broken-down, blasphemous wrecks of humanity, but with the very best that the world outside the Church can produce, and these we make our norm; these we must surpass; these inspire us.

Most important of all, he *challenges* us, this man outside the Church. As long as he exists he disturbs us, because his very existence casts doubt on the validity of our Christian experience. We have always taken it for granted that Christianity should be a witnessing religion and that in obedience to our Lord's commission we are bound to commend the Gospel to all men and, if possible, bring them into the Household of Faith. Are we going to make exceptions? Are we going to assume that because a person has achieved so much apart from the Gospel, he therefore has no need of the Gospel and can get along without the Church's message and fellowship in the way that a genius can get along without a formal education? If so, we reduce Christianity to what many of its critics would like to make it—a pink pill for personality problems, a crutch for weaklings and a refuge for the inadequate; the assumption being that if you are perfectly normal, if you have strength of character, you can get along without religion. The man outside the Church challenges us to explode that very misconception. Somehow we know that if we can reach him and commend our faith to him, then our faith must be sound and true and good. He challenges us simply because he is there, just as Mount Everest challenged adventurous men until they finally conquered it.

We have a duty to this man outside the Church, a duty which we evade by allowing him to believe that he represents the highest that man can achieve and that Christianity adds nothing to his life. To be sure, we find him difficult to approach. Talking to him about a Saviour seems like throwing a life-belt to a man sitting safely and comfortably on the seashore. He does not respond to the old arguments; emotional considerations have no appeal for him; but he is still a child of God, still a creature with a soul and therefore with hungers and longings that only God can satisfy. The great truth about the Roman Centurion was this: Christ could do something for him. Despite all his strength, all his innate qualities of character, he still reached a point of helplessness, a situation beyond his own ability to manage. He needed Christ, and in faith he turned to Christ with a dignified and humble trust unequalled even in the religious community of Israel. The finest man, simply because he is man and not God, needs God. Without God his life can never be complete, never achieve its highest potential. For the man he *is* outside the Church he commands our respect; or the man he *could be* within the family and household of God he commands our concern and our witness.

Sir Gordon Guggisberg was a man outside the Church. A Canadian of Swiss descent, he was intelligent, strikingly handsome and played cricket extremely well. As a brigadier general he served his country through the First World War with unique dedication and loyalty. After the war he became Governor of the Gold Coast of Africa. Sir Gordon felt no need of religion. On his shaving mirror he placed a card bearing the motto, "For God, for King, for Country." He said, "God meant nothing to me, the King meant a little, the Country everything." One day a gallant Christian said earnestly to the Governor, "You love your country because you have served it all your life; you have taken every opportunity of seeing the King; but you have never sought or even wished to know God." Himself a forthright man, Sir Gordon admired this forthright approach, and when he asked how one could know God, his friend replied, "Some of us believe that Jesus of Nazareth knew more of God than any other man, so we put aside some time each morning to study his thought of God and to let his Father speak to us." Guggisberg replied, "Damn it! I'll try. It's worth it if it's true." Six months later he was a convinced Christian, and through the succeeding years he gave his life to the service of the Africans whom he came to love. He founded a system of higher education for his people and became the most progressive Governor in all Africa. He died a poor man because he had given all his possessions to help his people.[1] But Sir Gordon Guggisberg proved something—he proved that even the strongest, most self-reliant and dedicated man outside the fellowship of Christ needs something that Christ can give him, and that when he becomes humble enough to accept it, his strength and influence are multiplied and transfigured.

[1] As told by Harold B. Walker in *The Power to Manage Yourself* (Harper and Brothers, Publishers, New York 1955), pp. 19–20

12

DESPISE YE THE CHURCH?

"... despise ye the Church of God?"

(1 Corinthians 11:22)

"... there were added that day about three thousand souls.
And they devoted themselves to the apostles' teaching and
fellowship, to the breaking of bread and the prayers."

(Acts 2: 41, 42)

LET US begin with Paul's sarcastic question to the Church
at Corinth, "Despise ye the Church of God?" There are
people in our day who would answer that question with
a resounding "Yes!" There are people who actually do hate
the Church and who would consider themselves bene-
factors of the human race if they could drive all churches
and parsons and priests and ecclesiastical institutions out of
existence. "Resolved that organized religion is the most
pernicious influence in modern society"—that was actually
the subject of a serious debate held in the London School of
Economics. Writes Bertrand Russell, "I say quite deliberately
that the Christian religion as organized in the churches has
been and still is the principal enemy of moral progress in
the world."

Others despise the Church rather in the manner that a
nouveau riche despises his poor relations; once he had use for
them, but now he has climbed above them in the social
scale, and finding them somewhat of an embarrassment, he
scarcely gives them a thought. About such people T. S. Eliot
wrote in these lines:

"I journeyed to London, to the timekept City,
Where the river flows, with foreign flotations.
There I was told: we have too many churches,
And too few chop-houses. There I was told

Let the vicars retire. Men do not need the Church
In the place where they work, but where they spend their
                                        Sundays.
In the City we need no bells:
Let them waken the suburbs.
I journeyed to the suburbs, and there I was told:
We toil for six days, and on the seventh we must motor
To Hindhead, or Maidenhead.
If the weather is foul we stay home and read the papers.
In industrial districts there I was told
Of economic laws.
In the pleasant countryside, there it seemed
That the country now is only fit for picnics.
And the Church does not seem to be wanted
In the country or in suburbs; and in the town
Only for important weddings."[1]

Still others despise the Church as a rather outmoded
and cumbersome and reactionary institution. They espouse
the cause of Christianity and they agree whole-heartedly
with what the churches are trying to say. They honestly
think that they themselves are leading Christian lives, but
so far as they are concerned, Christianity and the Church are
two separate things not necessarily related. They do not
believe that belonging to a church is an essential part of
being a Christian, nor do they believe that the organized
and visible Church in the world today authentically represents Christianity. Like the poet Swinburne, they express
admiration for Christ while despising his "leprous bride",
the Church. The great word on their lips is always the same,
"I don't have to go to church to be a Christian."

Assuming the sincerity of that point of view, we shall
attempt to answer it with an ancient and positive proposition: "No man can have God as his Father who does not
have the Church as his Mother." There is no vital, redemptive experience of Jesus Christ that does not include an experience of the Church which is the Body of Christ. As a basis
for this proposition we consult the New Testament and we
look specifically at the Day of Pentecost when the Spirit of

---

[1] T. S. Eliot, from *The Rock*, Faber and Faber Ltd., London 1934;
Harcourt, Brace and World, Inc., New York 1936

God descended upon his Church with supernatural power.
What actually happened that day has been helpfully illustrated by Bishop Lesslie Newbigin in his book, *The Household of God*.[1] He says that when a prospector first strikes oil,
there is often a violent eruption of the oil which sometimes
bursts into flames and burns for many days before it is
brought under control. Later on there will be no room for
such displays. The oil will be pumped through pipes and
refineries, man-made channels, to its destination, and what
began with a terrific display of power will settle down to a
steady, rather mundane, but productive, business.

There were fireworks on the Day of Pentecost—a sound
from heaven, the rush of mighty wind, tongues of fire, and
the Gospel of Christ proclaimed by "uneducated, common
men" in a chorus of many languages. All of this had a terrific
impact on the bystanders. They were witnessing a manifestation of Divine power and they knew it. They felt that God
had laid hold upon them irresistibly; they were filled with
a burning conviction. But what did they do about their conviction? A very ordinary thing, the New Testament tells us,
a thing so mundane that many people despise it. *They
joined the Church*. They realized that if their new and vital
experience of God were to be anything more than a mere
display of unharnessed energy, if it were to last and be productive, it must settle down and be directed through man-
made channels to its destination. So we read as the con-
cluding verse in the Pentecost story, ". . . there were added
(to the Church) that day about three thousand souls, and
they devoted themselves to the apostles' teaching and fellowship, to the breaking of bread and the prayers."

I

If we inquire into the reasons why the early Christians,
as a consequence of their religious experience, promptly
identified themselves with the Church's fellowship, we must
consider first that within the Church's fellowship *their experience of Christ had originated*. There could be no doubt

[1] S.C.M. Press, London 1953; Friendship Press, New York 1954.

about that. When God came to live upon the earth as a man, he surrounded himself immediately with a fellowship, and to this fellowship, not to isolated individuals, he gave the secrets of the Kingdom of God. To this fellowship he appeared after his resurrection and to this fellowship he entrusted the issues of his Kingdom; his disciples were to go forth and teach and to have authority over the powers of evil and to represent his Person in the fullest sense. Upon this fellowship the power of the Holy Spirit descended at Pentecost and out of this fellowship came the apostles and the missionaries who committed the Gospel to writing and carried the good news of salvation to the uttermost parts of the earth. Within this visible fellowship, not as a result of isolated influences, men came to know Christ; there they found themselves related to him as in no other way.

Our own lives bear a similar witness. Every man, when he reaches maturity, can look back and trace the various elements of his personality to certain sources. Obviously he owes the development of his mind, his formal knowledge and professional skills to his education in school and university. Perhaps he has a love of English literature, and this he owes to some magnetic teacher who taught the subject with competence and enthusiasm. Once he had the privilege of living for a few years in a foreign country, and ever since he has been a keen student of geography and languages and foreign cultures. Because he grew up in a large family, he has acquired the social graces, the ability to get along with people, to respect their rights and to tolerate their weaknesses. The child of idealistic parents, he has developed ideals, and though he may have rebelled against them in later adolescence, yet now he finds them deeply ingrained in his character. The poet who said "I am a part of all that I have met" spoke the essential truth about every man, for what is mature personality but a compound of the influences and experiences of our childhood and youth?

Our Christian experience originated in the Church. In a previous chapter we have recalled Zacchaeus, the Jewish tax-collector whom Jesus called down from the sycamore tree and to whose house he brought salvation. Legend has it that in later years Zacchaeus used to rise early every morning and carry a bucket of water to this tree and carefully water the roots. On one occasion his wife followed him, and when she asked the reason for this strange concern over an old sycamore tree, Zacchaeus replied, "This is where I found Christ." For nineteen centuries men have borne that same tender, affectionate witness concerning the Church, "This is where I found Christ—not on my own somewhere out in the world, but within the fellowship of Christians where God is worshipped, where the Word is preached and the Sacraments celebrated Sunday after Sunday. Where did I first meet Christ as my Lord and Saviour? I met him in a village church where the pews were hard and the music atrocious and I squirmed throughout the sermon, but where my parents came because they found strength there and where godly Sunday School teachers told me stories that I have never forgotten."

The man of the world may dispute that claim. He may say, "I consider myself a Christian, though neither I nor my parents ever darken the door of a church." His estimate of himself is probably untrue, but even if it were true, the man could not be a Christian unless someone at some time had darkened the door of a church. Whatever we possess of Christianity, whether we care for the Church or not, we have received from past generations who did care for the Church. We can no more escape the Church's influence than we can escape the influence of our own parents. We are surrounded on every hand by traditions that came out of the Church, by families whose roots are in the Church, by institutions and ideals that were born of the Church, and by men and women who believe in the Church and serve the Church. Apart from that direct or indirect influence there would be no Christianity in the world. We may despise the Church if we like, just as we may despise our own parents, but let us not then commit the blasphemy of claiming to be Christians, because we are despising the very origin of our Christianity, the one spiritual home in which men and women of all generations are brought to a knowledge of Jesus Christ as their Lord and Saviour.

Consider a second reason why the early Christians identified themselves with the Church. It was because they knew
that the Church's fellowship, being the origin of their
Christian experience, was also the soil in which *their experience of Christ could grow.* In a public park some children
were having great sport as they clambered over the trunk of
a tree which had been felled. I looked at this massive chunk
of wood and wondered how old it was and what would happen
to it now that it had been cut down for lumber. One thing
certain: its life as a tree was ended. It might become a handsome piece of furniture or a pew in a church or a communion table, but even as these it would eventually decay
and serve only as firewood. There was another tree in the
same park, a huge sycamore, its trunk ten feet across and its
spreading branches forming a natural umbrella that shaded
an area one hundred feet in diameter. It seemed much older
than the first tree, yet its leaves and fruit had all the freshness of a young sapling. Its great gnarled roots thrust themselves deep into the soil, drinking from the very bowels of the
earth the source of life that would keep it standing and
growing there for generations.

The first tree is a parable of our civilization, of a society
which gives the outward appearance of Christianity but
which, in despising the Church, has been uprooted from the
very source of life. As a Christian civilization our life has
ended, unless, like the second tree, we send our roots deep
into the soil of eternal spiritual values. That soil God has
provided in the Church which, though it may be shot through
with human ineptitude, still exists to remind men and women
of God and to proclaim the Gospel of their redemption.
When men despise the Church, they despise the one visible
institution that keeps alive the spiritual dimension in society,
the one institution founded on the belief that love has been
manifested as the ultimate meaning of the universe. Society
may turn its back on the Church and still be a Christian
society, just as lumber uprooted from the earth is still lumber,
but what a constricted and limited future it has compared

to the strength and the breadth of influence for which God intended it.

The early converts to Christianity, these men and women who witnessed the descent of the Holy Spirit at Pentecost, *might* not have joined the Church. They could have kept their religion a private affair; they had their burning conviction which would have sustained them for a long time. They knew, however, that their religious experience would neither grow nor survive indefinitely unless it were solidly rooted in the very soil whence it had sprung. Therefore they thrust their roots down deeply into "the apostles' teaching and fellowship, the breaking of bread and the prayers". They availed themselves, as every Christian must avail himself, of those things in the Church's life, its worship and prayer and preaching and sacrament, through which Christ continually imparts himself to us. Perhaps a man may be some kind of Christian outside the Church, but it is a rare person indeed who can be radiantly and decisively Christian without the means of grace which God has provided.

The greatest Christians—the saints, the martyrs, the reformers, the missionaries, those who have served the human race for the sake of Christ, and the quiet people who graced the common ways of life—have all been men and women who lived within the Church and whose impulse and inspiration came out of the Church's fellowship. There have been exceptions, of course, like Simone Weil, that remarkable Frenchwoman who, in obedience to Christ, toiled with farmers in the fields and workers in the factories, whose whole life was an oblation of service to her Lord and whose sacramental writings, especially about her sufferings, achieved heights of spirituality reached only by the great mystics. To the end of her life she remained outside the Church, not through indifference but by conviction; loyalty to Christ compelled her to remain outside the Church. Yet who has the strength or the grace to follow Simone Weil? because, as J. H. Oldham writes, after describing this remarkable Christian woman, "Take away the Church, and Christianity itself disappears. It is a delusion to suppose that we can cut out twenty centuries of lived experience and establish a direct relationship between ourselves and the historic Jesus".[1]

We can add to his words and say that Christianity is in its very heart and essence not a disembodied spirituality, but life in a visible fellowship. To despise the Church, to regard it as optional, as something which is purely instrumental to personal religious experience, a mere institution that may be altered, discarded or replaced, is to hold an undeveloped and distorted view of Christianity that in no way accords with the New Testament. The truth is that we need the Church; we need the Church's fellowship, we need the Church's ministry, we need the Church's teaching, we need the Church's sacrament. Just as the Church first introduced us to Jesus Christ as our Lord and Saviour, so the Church itself is the very soil in which our experience of Christ will grow.

III

Consider yet another reason why the early Christians identified themselves with the Church. It was because they knew that the Church's mission would provide them with the one significant means through which *their obedience to Christ could express itself*. Having accepted the Lordship of Jesus Christ, they knew that if they were to obey Christ and serve him, their witness must be through the visible fellowship which Christ himself had established. A man will say that he believes in Christianity, but not in the Church. Impossible! He might as well say that he believes in education but not in schools, in music but not in orchestras, in the labour movement but not in trade unions. There is no such thing as individual Christianity. Paul was a supreme individualist, by temperament an outsider, always rebelling against the policies of the fellowship; but Paul subjected himself to the discipline of the fellowship and he worked within the fellowship. It was the fellowship that sent him out as a missionary in the first place; and wherever Paul took the Gospel, he established fellowships, visible congregations to which he afterwards wrote his letters and

[1] *Life is Commitment* (S.C.M. Press, London 1953)

I

which became the nucleus of a world religion soon to prevail against the mightiest empire of antiquity.

Everybody has it on the tip of his tongue these days to tell us what is wrong with the Church. From television personalities to angry young men, from editorial writers to strangers on the street, you can solicit a chorus of criticisms telling you that the Church as an institution has failed; it has become irrelevant, outmoded, hopelessly removed from the real problems of real life in a real world. Some years ago a London newspaper offered a prize for the best essay on the subject, "What is wrong with the Church?" The prize was won by a minister from Wales who gave the answer: "What is wrong with the Church is our failure to realize and wonder at the beauty, the mystery, the glory and the greatness of the Church." We shall not deny that the Church has its imperfections, simply because it is a community of sinners and not of saints. Often the most loyal servants of the Church are those most tempted to lose faith in it and to seek a less inhibiting sphere of Christian obedience. But remember that Paul, when he asked his scathing question "Despise ye the Church of God?" was writing to the Christians themselves, the charter members of a little church at Corinth, whose very failure to realize and wonder at the beauty, the mystery, the glory and the greatness of the Church had brought the Church into disrepute.

Whoever despises the Church displays an abysmal ignorance of history. To be sure, much in the Church's history leaves room for regret, and there have been times when the Church, far from ennobling society, has contaminated it and plunged it into reaction and turmoil. But read the story in its wholeness and ask yourself if any single institution has played so decisive a rôle in the impulse to human freedom and dignity; the challenging of ignorance; the relief of suffering; the conquest of disease; the growth of humanitarian concern for the weak, the helpless, the destitute; the inspiration to great art and literature, architecture and music; the enlarging of personal horizons; the incentive to more sensitive and concerned moral living; the stabilizing of the inner lives of millions of people through the ages and around the world; the fostering of prophetic attacks by determined minorities on such giant evils as race prejudice, economic exploitation and war. You cannot tell the story of the past two thousand years and leave the Church's influence out. For all its human bungling and blundering, the Church has been and still remains the supremely creative transforming force in human life and the world.

People who despise the Church have no imagination. They need to visualize our society as it would fast become if all people were as indifferent to the churches as they are, so that the churches had to close their doors for lack of support. Imagine it—a society deprived of its major character-building agency, the one institution that exists to remind men that they are created sons of God and therefore subject to his laws and his sovereignty. Imagine society deprived of the well-spring of human charity, the one institution that does see every man as a child of God and exists to bind broken hearts, to raise the fallen and recover the lost. Imagine society deprived of its one source of hope, the one institution that exists to remind men that though they may have lost control of their world, God has not lost control of it. God created this world in love and he rules it in love. He redeemed it in love, and by raising Christ from the dead he demonstrated conclusively that no concentration of evil can pluck the world out of his eternal purpose. Imagine society deprived of its one agent of reconciliation, the one institution that exists to reconcile men to God and therefore to one another. "Now I happen to believe," said one of America's great theologians, "that in cold, realistic, practical terms, the best hope for world civilization lies in the Christian Church. Despite its divisions, its stuffiness, its slowness, its enslavement to nationalistic prejudices, social conservatism and rigid dogma, the Church is mankind's most effective instrument for restoring mutual confidence, for instilling contrition, for allaying anxiety, and for opposing fanatical will-to-power. . . ."[1]

"Despise ye the Church *of God*?" In the last analysis, how

[1] David E. Roberts, *The Grandeur and Misery of Man* (Oxford University Press, New York 1955)

can you despise the Church without despising God himself? The Church was not man's idea, a community creation like a political party, a labour union, a service club or a public school. The Church came into being not because a group of high-minded do-gooders decided that there should be one, but because the Lord said, "I will build my Church, and the gates of hell shall not prevail against it." In all its teaching, the New Testament makes it unremittingly clear that Christ and his Church are one and indivisible; there can be no relationship to one outside the other; no Church —no Christ. When the early theologians framed the historic creeds to articulate the faith once delivered to the saints, they put their belief in the Church on the very same basis as their belief in Father, Son and Holy Spirit, implying that no man can say, "I believe in the Christian God," unless he can also say, "I believe in the Christian Church." The Church is God's creation; he called it into being and he equipped it as the spiritual home in which we should come to know Christ as Lord and Saviour, as the soil in which our experience of Christ should grow, as the means through which our obedience to Christ should find expression. "No man can have God as his Father who does not have the Church as his Mother." That is why the first Christians "devoted themselves to the apostles' teaching and fellowship, to the breaking of bread and the prayers". If you believe in the Christ of God, you will believe also in the Church of God. If you claim to be a Christian at all, you will know that your place is in the Church.

13

THREE PHILOSOPHIES OF LIFE

"But a certain Samaritan, as he journeyed, came where he was: and when he saw him, he had compassion on him, and went to him, and bound up his wounds, pouring in oil and wine ... and brought him to an inn, and took care of him."

(St. Luke 10: 33–34)

Next to the Prodigal Son the story of the Good Samaritan is the most familiar of our Lord's parables. Entirely unsophisticated, it conceals no theological profundities, no hidden allegories. It is a lesson in ethical behaviour; in simplest terms it tells people how they should live together; it is a word-picture of the responsible society.

Some twenty years ago there was an interesting little radio drama built around the story of the Good Samaritan. According to this modernized version the Jericho authorities decided to do something about the case of the assaulted Jew, so they turned over to the first-century Scotland Yard the responsibility of tracking down the robbers and the witnesses involved in the incident. Coming to the scene of the crime, the investigators discovered some clearly marked footprints in the sand. They saw in each footprint the trademark of the firm which had manufactured the sandals. Questioning these sandal makers, they found three different trademarks which had been worn respectively by the robbers, the priest and the Levite, and the Good Samaritan, and each trademark revealed a clue to a very distinct philosophy of life.

I

First, the robbers. They wore sandals the soles of which had been stamped with the motto, *"What's Yours is Mine.*

133

I'll take it!" This was their philosophy of life, and they made no apology for it, no effort to disguise it with any cloak of respectability. Thieving was their business, their full-time profession. The property which other people accumulated by honest skill and labour—this the robbers counted fair game, to be taken by violence if necessary. They had nothing personal against the poor fellow whom they attacked on the Jericho Road; he just happened to be the victim of their philosophy.

According to newspaper reports an investigation into robbery in London has been undertaken by the new Cambridge Institute of Criminology. We learn to our alarm that robberies are turning "more professional". In 1950 there were ninety-five major robberies in London. In 1957 the number rose to one hundred and seventy-four. It was estimated that in 1960 there would be three hundred and forty-four cases of major theft. The number of all robberies between 1950 and 1959 shows an increase of one hundred and sixty-one per cent.

All this reminds us that every generation breeds its Jericho Road robbers, human parasites who have no respect for the property rights of others. From petty pilferers to big-time racketeers, they live by their wits or their fists, and to protect ourselves against them we build prisons and maintain police forces. Indeed, so brilliantly do some modern thieves operate, that if they turned their ingenuity and skill to the business of earning an honest living, many of them might be successful and wealthy. Honesty has no fascination for them, however, no challenge. They steal as a matter of principle; they live by the philosophy, "What's Yours is Mine. I'll take it!"

In North America some philanthropic groups employ gambling enterprises to raise money for worthy causes. Bingo and other games of chance attract thousands of people, many of whom can ill afford it, but all consumed by the passion to transfer money from other people's pockets to their own. Commenting on this craze in a magazine article,[1]

[1] "Hurricane Bingo", by Francis Emmett Williams (*Christian Century*, June 15, 1955)

an American County Court Judge notes that there are five levels on which we may operate to acquire property: (1) Market price, a fair exchange; something for something one hundred per cent. (2) Investment. Something for something at long range; honest and legal. (3) Speculation; something for nothing in many cases; runs all the way from the legal to the illegal and often shades over into gambling. (4) Gambling; something for nothing ninety-nine per cent; usually illegal; it was classed by the ancient Hebrews as robbery and by the Hindus as the equivalent of theft. (5) Stealing; something for nothing one hundred per cent; illegal anywhere. In other words, says Judge Williams, "When you pay one dollar for a chance to win a hundred dollars, your desire to get the property of others by chance and without paying for it clicks at ninety-nine per cent— else you wouldn't do it. Stated briefly, the difference between the motivation in promoted gambling and pickpocket thievery is consent and one per cent." Judge Williams terms gambling "robbery by mutual consent", but still robbery, just as duelling is murder by mutual consent, but still murder. Define it as you may, every gambling enterprise, however respectable, however worthy the cause to which it is harnessed, operates on the principle, "What's Yours is Mine. I'll take it!"

Unspeakable tragedy flows from the abnormal criminal covetousness of this first philosophy of life. All through history on a world scale it has been true, as great powers have conquered little nations, stolen their territory, appropriated their resources and taxed them to a point of bankruptcy and starvation. Consider the brutalities of *laissez-faire* capitalism. A hundred years ago the coal barons made themselves wealthy by sending little children to toil underground in the mines for thirteen hours a day. Fortunes have been amassed on what has been stolen from people, not in money, but in time, brains, brawn and labour. Now the pendulum has swung to the opposite extreme, and in all parts of the world, America no less than Britain, we have a creeping socialism which presses for a fairer distribution of wealth and natural resources. The welfare state is here to stay, and no one questions its immense benefits; yet the welfare state must be recognized as a mixed blessing when it destroys personal initiative and engenders in people the illusion that society owes them a living. After reading the parable of the Good Samaritan, a Sunday School teacher asked one of the children what he had learned from it. He replied, "I have learned that when I get into trouble, someone should help me out." Exactly. "What's Yours is Mine!"

II

We return to our first-century investigators. Studying the opposite side of the road from the scene of the crime, they found footprints made by sandals of a more expensive variety. Manufactured in Jerusalem, they had been worn by a priest and a Levite, and they, too, left a motto imprinted in the sand, another philosophy of life. *"What's Mine is Mine. I'll keep it!"*

In some respects these men deserve more condemnation than the robbers. At least the latter made no pretence at being anything but robbers. But the priest and the Levite were solid citizens; religious professionals, in fact. They of all people should have been moved to compassion by the sight of a fellow-countryman lying senseless at the roadside, and they should have stopped to help him. Of course, they may have been in a hurry. Perhaps they were on their way to a committee meeting. I have always suspected that when the Devil wants to render a man useless as a channel of vital thought and constructive action, he simply bogs him down with an unreasonable number of committee meetings. You have heard the definition of a camel: "a horse designed by a committee". In this case it may have been a charitable enterprise, some project to "clean up the Jericho Road", and render more effective service to the victims of robbers. At any rate, like most committee meetings, the resolutions would be comfortably impersonal, broad principles and general reforms, rather than specific imperatives affecting the members themselves in their own philosophy of life.

No self-respecting person admires the priest and the

Levite. One wag suggests that in reading the parable we change our emphasis to say, "And when they saw that he *had* been robbed, they passed by on the other side." At the same time, we hesitate to throw stones. It is, after all, a man's own decision what he does with that which legitimately belongs to him. If he wants to share with the wounded at his roadside, well and good; but he should not be intimidated into it. "What's Mine is Mine. I'll keep it!" The great majority of people live by this philosophy, and they resent it bitterly when the Church or the government or anyone else steps in and begins dictating to them about the disposition of their own property. A man builds up a business the hard way, starts on a small scale, sacrifices sleep and pleasure, battles his competitors, achieves success. Such a man is bound to become careful and cautious, bound to react indignantly when people less industrious than himself reach out to grab his valuable time and hard-earned money. "What's Mine is Mine. I'll keep it!" Not the most admirable philosophy of life, but there is surely nothing wrong with it.

Nothing wrong, except that it is simply not true. Essentially you have to become an atheist in order to believe it. You have to leave God out of your calculations altogether. You have to dismiss as fantastic the great Biblical doctrines of Creation, Providence and Redemption and commit yourself to a totally materialistic, mechanistic and humanistic view of life and the universe. When you can look through a telescope at the constellations, or through a microscope at the life sperm, and say, "These are the work of my hands"; when you can behold the treasures of ocean, forest and mine and say, "I have it within my power to provide these things"; when you can cancel out all the riches of our Judeo-Christian civilization, the cultural and spiritual heritage of the ages, and say, "I have no need of this"— then only will you be speaking the truth as you assert arrogantly, "What's Mine is Mine. I'll keep it!"

No, there is nothing wrong with this philosophy of life except that it wrecks our human relationships. Marriages collapse because people enter them reservedly and because

one or both partners holds something back, a private
sanctuary into which the other is not allowed to trespass. In
their old age people find themselves lonely and friendless
because all their lives they have lived selfishly, shutting out
their neighbours and caring for no one but themselves. The
world may blow itself to hell one of these days, and if that
final catastrophe happens, the fault will lie not with inter-
national robbers, but with international adolescents who
have an exaggerated sense of their own property rights,
their own racial and economic privileges, and who cling to
them jealousy and protect them with iniquitous legislation.

Consider what this selfish philosophy does to the soul.
Dostoyevski wrote a classic story about a woman who died
and was consigned to eternal torment. In her agony she
cried out for mercy. At length an angel answered, "I can
help you if you can remember one altogether unselfish thing
you did while on earth." It seemed easy, but when she began
to recite her good deeds, she realized that every one of them
had been done from a motive of self-interest. Finally, at the
point of despair, she remembered a carrot she had once
given to a beggar. She feared to mention it, because it had
been a poor withered carrot that she would never have
used in the stew she was preparing. But the angel consulted
the record, and the record showed that the act had been
prompted by unselfishness, not great unselfishness or it
would have been a better gift, but unselfishness none the
less. So down the limitless space that separates heaven from
hell the carrot was lowered on a slender string. Could this
weak thing bear her weight and lift her out of torment? It
did not seem possible, but desperation made her try. She
grasped the withered carrot and slowly began to rise. Then
she felt a weight dragging at her. She looked down and saw
other tormented souls clinging to her, hoping to escape with
her. "Let go! Let go!" she cried. "The carrot won't hold us
all!" But grimly, desperately, they held on. Again she cried,
"Let go! This is *my* carrot!" At that point the string broke,
and, still clutching the carrot she had reclaimed for herself, the woman fell back into the pains of hell. This
sums up the fate of anyone who lives by the philosophy,

"What's Mine is Mine!" In the long run he gets the carrot, nothing more.

III

Then these first-century investigators of the Jericho Road robbery found another set of trademarks which they traced to a sandal maker up in Samaria. Stamped on the bottom of the sandals worn by the Good Samaritan were words which expressed his philosophy of life, *"What's Mine is Yours. I'll share it."*

Consider the extent of this man's generosity. First, he was a Samaritan. You know what that meant. The Jews had no dealings with the Samaritans. Had their rôles been reversed and the Samaritan been beaten by robbers, probably the Jew would not have lifted a finger to help him. Second, he exposed himself to danger. No one, least of all a foreigner, took pleasure-trips down the brigand-infested Jericho Road. Moving along with cautious rapidity, he only drew attention to himself by stopping to help this poor fellow at the roadside. Third, he rendered a personal service. Doubtless he could have rushed into the city and notified some relief agency; instead he dirtied his own hands, dressed the man's wounds, cleansed and soothed them with wine and oil and lifted him on to his own donkey. Fourth, he gave generously of his time; took the Jew, not ahead, but back to the inn, got him safely lodged and delayed his own journey almost twenty-four hours to remain overnight and attend personally to the man's needs. Finally, all of this cost him something—an extra night's lodging for himself as well as for the wounded Jew, plus money and a credit card which he gave the innkeeper to take care of the poor victim. Do you wonder that we call him the "Good" Samaritan? Such acts of extravagant kindness do not happen spontaneously. They can only articulate a basic philosophy of life, "What's Mine is Yours. I'll share it."

I read somewhere that the world's hungry people, arranged in single file, would form a line extending around the globe twenty-five times. Never has our Lord's parable been so relevant to the human situation as it is today; never have we seen so clearly the challenge and the opportunity to cast ourselves as a Christian society in the rôle of the Good Samaritan. In this twentieth century there is at least one unmistakable counterpart of the wounded victim lying at the roadside—the political refugee who has been attacked and beaten by some bullying power, stripped of his country and his home, tossed on the side of the road and left there, half dead. Since 1945 at least forty million persons have crossed frontiers, artificial or traditional, looking for asylum and sustenance. These are men without a country, without political or economic status, living on the edge of starvation and reduced to the privacy of a strung blanket. It is estimated that in India one person in forty-two is a refugee, in Viet Nam one in twelve, in Pakistan one in eleven, in Korea one in three, and in Hong Kong nearly two in seven. In the Middle East two hundred thousand children have been born refugees. The refugee problem is a massive crime against humanity, the greatest single issue facing the world of our time. A few governments and a few voluntary agencies have done their best, but we shall never begin to confront this problem on a realistic and imaginative scale until we change our whole philosophy of life to accord with the teachings of Jesus in the New Testament.

So the Jericho Road girdles the globe. That means that it passes our front door and that right where we live there may be poor, unfortunate people who have been beaten down by the circumstances of life and who lie in the ditch desperately needing our help. Some have economic needs— money to pay off their debts, employment that will yield sufficient income to finance the necessities for themselves and their families. Others need friendship, because they care for no one and they feel that no one cares for them; they are the victims of loneliness, of the vast, impersonal, mechanized nature of our city living. Others have spiritual needs. Their own appetites and passions tyrannize them; they are the victims of their own moods; a feeling of futility bullies their souls, and they have nothing permanent and stable to which they can cling. All of these people will die unless someone stops to help them, unless someone from the abundance of his own resources, material and spiritual, reaches out hands of mercy and says, "I have what you need. What's Mine is Yours. I'll share it."

There is One who does come to the sufferer in his need, One who upon this earth fulfilled the pattern of the Good Samaritan. Jesus gave. His time, energies, material possessions, insights, capacities, sympathy—Jesus gave them all to all sorts and conditions of men. He held nothing back, kept nothing for himself. At times he felt the awful weariness of one who spends himself for others, but he followed the path of self-giving to the place where it takes every man eventually—a lonely cross outside a city wall. It was no fictitious figure that Jesus portrayed in his timeless parable, but a portrait of himself as he lived and died upon this earth and as he comes to us now in his living presence. "What's Mine is Yours. I'll share it!" It is no academic theory to which our Lord calls us, but a real, concrete philosophy of life tried and tested and found workable in the rough arena of human experience.

14

THE PRINCIPLE OF NONCONFORMITY

"Do not be conformed to this world but be transformed by the renewal of your mind, that you may prove what is the will of God, what is good and acceptable and perfect."

(Romans 12 : 2)

IT IS time we revised the meaning of the word "nonconformist". As an ecclesiastical concept it has outlived its usefulness. Nonconformity presupposes conformity, an organic relationship between the state and some particularly favoured church, and that simply does not exist in the New World. In England it now exists in little more than name only; although the Anglican Church is still the Established Church, and while one may derive certain social advantages by conforming to it, one is not pressured by law to conform or penalized for refusing to conform.

Of course, we know that this is a comparatively recent development and that a vastly different picture obtained three hundred years ago when Charles II ascended the throne. Charles hated all Protestants. During his reign and subsequent to it Parliament enacted a series of decrees reducing non-Anglicans, or "Dissenters" as they were called, to the status of second-class citizens. The Schism Act prohibited anyone from teaching in a school unless he were a communicant of the Church of England; and not until 1871 were nonconformists admitted to the ancient English universities. By the Test Act all civil or military officers must take the oath of supremacy and allegiance and receive the Lord's Supper according to the usages of the Church of England. One paid a heavy price in those days for being a nonconformist, and we can well understand that while many suffered heroically for their principles, others, to advance their political ambitions or get their children into college, compromised and became what were called "occasional conformists". As one Lord Mayor of London remarked, a few masses were a small price to pay for his chains of office. But who can blame Englishmen of the seventeenth and eighteenth centuries for yielding to the pressures of the social order in which they had to live? We might have done the same. We can thank God that the nineteenth century saw these infamous Acts repealed and that in most non-Roman Catholic countries today the concept of religious conformity has fallen into disuse.

So let us divest the word "nonconformist" of its ecclesiastical dress and let us reclothe it with its Biblical meaning. "Do not be conformed to this world," writes Paul in the twelfth chapter of his Epistle to the Romans. Paul's Roman Letter, that most mature and reasoned statement of the Christian Faith, takes us into the very heart of the Gospel; it proclaims the good news that "the law of the Spirit of life in Jesus Christ has set us free from the law of sin and death". Because of what God has done for our salvation in Christ, and because we believe in Christ, we now are sons of God, members of a new order of life and righteousness, and we have to live lives appropriate to that order. But this presents problems, as the readers of Paul's Roman Letter knew only too well. Redeemed from paganism, they nevertheless continued to live and work and do business in a pagan environment; they were a small, unpopular minority pressured by the ostracism of family and friends and the constant threat of the Imperial power. It was not easy to be a Christian in first-century Rome. Every day you were tempted to fall back into the old ways, to continue being a Christian in name only, and in practice to conform to the world about you as if nothing had happened.

Therefore—Paul follows his proclamation of the Gospel with that stout word, "therefore"—the basic principle of the Christian life is a principle of nonconformity. "Do not be conformed to this world. . . ." As a Word of God it speaks with peculiar force to Christians of every age whatever their ecclesiastical tradition. It warns us, as Karl Barth warned the Reformed Churches in Hungary, that true Christianity always moves "against the stream". The true follower of Christ will live in a state of tension with his environment, like a stranger exiled in a foreign country. Constantly he will feel the pressure to camouflage his identity, to soft-pedal his uniqueness, and, for the sake of expediency, to conform to the world about him. Instead of standing over against the pagan culture and judging it, he will be tempted to identify himself with that culture and to reflect the intellectual and social and moral climate of the age. Distinctive for his beliefs and his piety, he may yet live such a worldly life as to earn the cynical remark of a modern poet, "These Christians do it every Sunday. They'll be all right on Monday. It's just a little habit they've acquired." "Do not be conformed to this world. . . ." Four considerations suggest themselves as we ponder this basic principle of the Christian life.

I

Consider, first, that *we live in an age of conformity*. Some months ago a newspaper carried an article bemoaning the so-called "globocracy" induced by the swiftness of modern transportation and communication. The nations, it declared, are becoming monotonously similar. In the not-too-distant future peoples all over the world will be dressing more alike, eating the same foods, living in a few standard types of houses, watching the same international television programmes, dancing the same dances, responding to the same advertisements, developing the same tastes.

Standardization has already become the prevailing feature in Western society. We see it in commonplace things like clothing fashions which prevail on both sides of the Atlantic according to the dictates of the Paris dress designers. We see it in more serious things like the emergence of stereotyped ideas and opinions, the mass mind moulded by the press, radio and television, films and book clubs. More and more we are urged to conform until individuality of expression and independence of judgment are in danger of becoming lost arts. A man ceases to be a man; before your hypnotized

gaze he changes into a type whose personality, clothes, automobile, brains and wife are completely interchangeable with
thousands of others of his type.

Conformity dominates many of the social institutions of
our time. It is the very ethos of Communism, a political
system which now claims half the earth's population and
operates on the premise that man is not an individual with
a mind of his own, but a soulless cog in the machinery of the
State. Behind the Iron Curtain you either conform, or
else. . . ! The antithesis should be democracy, but democracy also can produce the mob-mind, a band-wagon
mentality that keeps everybody in line and discourages free
and independent judgment. Conformity becomes the corner-
stone in some systems of education, schools and colleges
dedicated to the production of bricks and parrots instead of
educated men and women who can think for themselves.
Even religion, despite the fact that Whitehead described it as
"what a man does with his solitariness", can be socialized
and suffocated by an ecclesiastical authoritarianism that
intimidates men to make them conform.

"Do not be conformed to this world." More subtly does
the world pressure the soul of a Christian today than it did
in ancient Rome, simply because the Christian contends not
with outright paganism but with something more insidious
—a nominal Christian society that often exists with no
reference to God's will. Dr. C. F. von Weizsäcker quietly
teaches philosophy at the University of Tübingen in Germany. Few people know that Professor von Weizsäcker is a
distinguished nuclear physicist who, in obedience to Christian
convictions, turned his back on the scientific laboratory. In
1958 he said in an address to the Central Committee of the
World Council of Churches, "I cannot see how I personally
could in any way take part in making or using atomic bombs.
This is not a thing I have known for all times. I was an atomic
scientist during the war, and at that time I was working on
the problem of nuclear energy. . . . Of course, that means that
I am prepared to accept the consequences of my decision for
my own person, for my family and for my nation, whatever
these consequences may be." Had this great German so

dramatically dissociated himself from some obvious evil, like the publication of obscene literature, we should, no doubt, applaud his courage, but because he has turned his back on pursuits which many consider essential to man's survival, and therefore righteous, we shake our heads and regard him as an eccentric. Society deals harshly with its nonconformists. It was a cynical man, but a realist, who replied when asked by a youth the secret of success, "Conform, my boy, conform. Never mind your personal convictions. Stand with the majority. Do what your superiors tell you. And, above all, don't try to change anything!"

II

This leads to a second consideration, namely, that *it takes courage to be a nonconformist*. We have within us such irresistible forces driving us toward conformity. The imitative instinct is powerful. We are all influenced in thought and behaviour, more than we care to admit, by what other people think and do. To her horror a mother found her small boy engaged in the painful process of pulling his thick hair out by the roots. She stopped him at once and asked the reason for this strange behaviour. Innocently he replied, "I want to be like Dr. Jones." Dr. Jones (and I have purposely changed his name) was the dearly beloved and greatly idolized minister of the church which this family attended, and Dr. Jones was as bald as a billiard ball. At least the little fellow was not trying to imitate Yul Brynner; he was merely trying to keep up with the Joneses. The advertisers capitalize on this imitative instinct which few of us outgrow. With their new "depth psychology" they appeal to our envy, our covetousness, our insane desire to keep up with the Joneses and to imitate the so-called Men and Women of Distinction.

We have the gregarious instinct, too, the fear of being different. I came across this sentence from a novel, "He wanted passionately to be indistinguishable on the surface from other men. . . ." What an apt description of that great army of young men walking the streets of New York in their grey flannel suits, or the streets of London in their striped trousers and bowler hats, men who think and live and act according to the dictates of custom, their manner of dress decided by the fashion or fad of the day, their conversation composed of conventional clichés, their pleasures determined by unimaginative amusement-makers who invent some stupid vogue in entertainment or resurrect some antique diversion and adorn it in modern disguise. Many people live by the herd instinct; they have a dread of being different; their first and final justification for behaviour is the silly statement, "Everybody is doing it."

The security instinct drives us to conformity. It may not be dignified, but at least it is safe to be swept along in the stream of other people's ideas and opinions. Three years ago my wife and I travelled by train down the Rhine Valley in the same compartment with a young German who insisted on paying for our breakfast, because he felt so indebted to my country and to others for standing between West Germany and Communism. Harold Walker, in his book *The Power to Manage Yourself*,[1] tells of a similar experience. He also travelled by train down the Rhine Valley and struck up a conversation with a young, educated, intelligent German sitting in the same compartment. This man recalled his years as a Hitler Brown Shirt, helping to take the nation by storm. Then he remarked, "A hundred times since the war I have wondered why I did what I did. I betrayed every ideal I ever had. I violated my deepest convictions. Why? I simply was swept along with the crowd. It was the safest thing to do in those days."

Charles Kingsley once wrote an open letter to the young men of his parish. It began:

"My dear young men: The human race may for practical purposes be divided into three divisions. First, the honest men who mean to do right and do it. Second, the knaves who mean to do wrong and do it. Third, the fools who mean to do whichever of the two is pleasanter at the moment. And these last may be divided into black fools and white fools. The black fools are they who would rather do wrong than right, but dare not unless it is the fashion; while the white fools are they who

[1] Harper and Brothers, Publishers (New York 1955), p. 127

would rather do right than wrong, but dare not unless it is the fashion."

"Do not be conformed to this world. . . ." It takes courage to resist conformity. Young people especially feel that they must satisfy the requirements of sociability; they dread being different from other people; they wish to be congenial and acceptable; they would like to be popular. At Aberdeen University there is an inscription, THEY SAY. WHAT DO THEY SAY? LET THEM SAY. A noble declaration of moral independence, but it takes the highest and rarest form of courage to say it and mean it. It takes courage to say "No" when everyone else is saying "Yes" and to say "Yes" when everyone else is saying "No". Once a man was crucified because he swam upstream while all others were swimming down, and to some extent whoever dares to be a nonconformist will carry a Cross.

III

Nevertheless, we must also consider that *nonconformists are the makers of history*. Voltaire once remarked that every man is either the hammer or the anvil, one who strikes or one who is struck. Every man is either a creator of fact or a creature of circumstance, one who puts colour into his environment, or, like a chameleon, takes his colour from the environment. Someone has found the same parallel in a comparison between thermometers and thermostats.[1] The thermometer reveals, records and registers the temperature; it conforms completely to the environmental situation; its behaviour is definitely determined from without. The thermostat has the same characteristics plus one significant factor, the element of control. It is not the environment that determines the thermostat, but the thermostat that determines the environment.

These are the two basic principles of earthly existence; call them the principles of survival and progress. The thermo-

[1] Henry Hitt Crane, *Thermometers versus Thermostats*, in *Great Preaching Today*, ed. by Alton M. Motter (Harper and Brothers, Publishers, New York 1955), p. 30ff.

metric principle characterizes all sub-human life, as biologists since Darwin have made clear. Organisms of the lower order, plants and animals, survive largely by their capacity to adjust themselves to their surroundings, to be adaptable and flexible, to change their very nature if necessary. Man, on the other hand, has within him a new factor—control. More than a creature, he is potentially a co-creator. Instead of being conformed to this world, he can transform it. Refusing to be determined by his environment, he can determine what his environment shall be. He is not a thermometer but a thermostat. This is the distinguishing characteristic of man, the Divine in him, the quality that raises him above the brutes. Let him surrender this quality, and he reverts to the status of brutes; let him exercise it, and he has the power to shape history.

The future has always belonged to the nonconformists. In all generations the strong characters, the leaders, the men who most effectively directed the destinies of their fellowmen, were the nonconformists who, careless of their own safety, defied public opinion and dared to stand alone. Five centuries before Christ a Hebrew prophet named Jeremiah branded himself "Public Enemy Number One", because he stood at the gate of the temple and counselled a course of political action that savoured of cowardice and treason. Today the only authentic history of that stormy period comes to us in a book that bears his name. Two thousand years later, Martin Luther, a Roman monk, a man so brilliant that he might have been a cardinal had he silenced his doubts and sensibly conformed to authority, blazoned his doubts and convictions abroad, and when ordered to recant before civil and ecclesiastical powers, replied with the rallying cry of the Protestant Reformation, "Here I stand! I cannot do otherwise! God help me!"

The saviours of mankind have been the nonconformists. Most people are like chips of wood swept along the stream of life until eventually they find their way into a stagnant pool where they remain until they rot. But every now and then a generation produces a swimmer who fights his way upstream, who refuses to go along with the crowd, not a creature of circumstance but a creator of fact, whose life releases such power that he transforms the moral atmosphere and changes an entire community. He may not be a great man, important in terms of worldly standards. He may be an ordinary human being like Desmond Barry, whose inspiring story appeared in the *Reader's Digest* (November 1958). To appreciate his story, you must understand that the most irresistible social force in America today is the labour union. Though a particular union may be rotten to the core, the employer must go along with it if he wants to survive. But not Desmond Barry who owns a small trucking company in Houston, Texas. When the powerful Teamsters' Union threw a contract on his desk and ordered him to sign, he insisted that his drivers should join the union of their choice. The Teamsters didn't argue; they promptly attacked Barry with their effective weapon, "economic blackmail", boycotting his cargo and making impossible the continued co-operation of trucking companies in other states. Barry hired a lawyer and began fighting the so-called "hot-cargo" clause in the courts. Then his customers began dropping away. When he persisted in the fight, vandals invaded his truck yards and smashed his vehicles. It took him two years and near bankruptcy to win his case, but at the time when the magazine article was written he was on his feet again, and a glimmer of hope now shines in the dark valley of labour relations because of one energetic and courageous employer who refused to conform.

IV

Consider finally that *nonconformity is nothing less than the religious experience of conversion*. "Do not be conformed to this world. . . ." This is not a plea for mere eccentricity, or mere stubbornness. There is, after all, such a thing as unredeemed nonconformity. Hugh MacLennan's novel, *The Watch that Ends the Night*, is not a great novel because there are no great characters in it, but it is an absorbing story, brilliantly written. Its leading character, Jerome Martel, is a gifted surgeon whose abnormal childhood and experiences in the First War have made him a passionate nonconformist. He simply cannot adjust. He tangles with the protocol of his profession and has a sense of involvement in human misery which allows him to become an innocent dupe in the hands of local Communists. Eventually he leaves Canada and sails for Spain to alleviate suffering in the Spanish Civil War, but he does it at the expense of his vocation as a surgeon and his duty as a husband and father.

"Do not be conformed to this world. . . ." For the Christian, nonconformity means something more positive and profound than a passion for peculiarity. Let Paul complete his basic principle of the Christian life. "Do not be conformed to this world, but be transformed by the renewal of your mind, that you may prove what is the will of God, what is good and acceptable and perfect." Something has taken place in the experience of a Christian, something supernatural and decisive. By his faith in Christ, his willingness to be the one whom Christ has redeemed, he has been born again, ushered into a whole new order of existence upon this earth. Therefore he must live the life of that order, and that means inward renewal, a transformation of his mind, a complete reorientation of his thinking to accord with the controlling principle of that new order which is the will of God. No longer is he the slave of conventional judgments, for he now has a fresh and independent insight into moral realities. One and only one criterion determines his convictions and his conduct: Do they accord with the will of God? Are they good in themselves, satisfying and complete?

Having said that, Paul becomes very practical, and with his usual concreteness goes on to describe the character of a Christian nonconformist. It is really a description of the character of Christ. Read it, and ask yourself if the man who fulfils it does not, even today, stand apart from his fellows, over against the accepted customs and convictions of our world.

" The nonconformist," writes Paul, "loathes evil and clings to the good. He loves the brethren and seeks to outdo them in showing honour. He never flags in Christian zeal, is aglow in the Spirit, serves the Lord. He is joyful in hope, stands firm in trouble, and persists in prayer. He contributes to the needs of

God's people and practises hospitality. He blesses those who persecute him, blesses and does not curse. He rejoices with those who rejoice and weeps with those who weep. He lives in harmony with the brethren. He is not haughty, but associates with humble folk. He is never conceited. He does not pay back evil for evil. He is guided by what all men count honourable. He tries to live at peace with all men. He never avenges himself, but loves even an enemy according to the Scriptures which say, 'If your enemy is hungry, feed him; if he is thirsty, give him drink.' The nonconformist is never conquered by evil; he overcomes evil with good."

That is what Paul means by Christian nonconformity— a complete change of mind and heart, so that we think and behave no longer according to the manner and standard of the world but according to the will of God. We ourselves cannot effect this dramatic reorientation in our lives. Nonconformity in the Christian sense must be the work of the Holy Spirit within us, a miracle of Divine Grace, nothing less than the religious experience of conversion. We cannot cultivate it but we can pray for it. We cannot achieve it but we can receive it. God, who in Christ has delivered us from the kingdom of darkness and transferred us to the Kingdom of his beloved Son, will, by the power of his Holy Spirit, renew, refashion and remould our lives in harmony with that Divine Kingdom.

15

TURNING THE WORLD UPSIDE DOWN

> ". . . they dragged some of the brethren before the city authorities, crying, 'These men who have turned the world upside down have come here also.' "
>
> (Acts 17 : 6)

IN THE second century a pagan writer named Celsus attacked the Church for its other-worldliness. He said, "Christians appear to me like a host of bats or ants who come out of their hiding-places, or like frogs who sit in a swamp, or worms who hold a meeting in the corner of a manure pile and say to one another, 'To us God reveals and proclaims everything. He does not trouble himself with the rest of the world; we are the only beings with whom he has dealings.' "

It was an absurd accusation with no foundation in fact whatever. Had the early Christians been content to survive as the Roman described them, a secret society that held aloof from the world, then the bloody history of the martyrs would never have been written, for the world would have had no argument with Christianity. Precisely because these grubs and insects emerged from their filthy hiding-places and penetrated all areas of man's common life, they were branded a menace to public safety to be crushed and exterminated and wiped off the face of the earth. God not trouble himself with the rest of the world? Long before the chin of Celsus boasted a beard, the followers of Jesus Christ had been dragged before kings and magistrates and sentenced to death as "men who have turned the world upside down".

The word "world" appears more than two hundred times in the New Testament. It was a favourite word of Paul. Jesus used it often; he made it the theme of his High Priestly

Prayer in the Upper Room. Repeatedly the Gospels and Epistles come to grips with the problem of the Church and the world, the relationship of the Christian community and of the Christian himself to the immediate environment.

It would appear that certain New Testament passages conceive the world to be Satan's territory, estranged from God and therefore at enmity with the Church, an evil domain to be guarded against and renounced and fought to the death. In the Parable of the Soils, Jesus talks about the thorns, "the cares of this world"—not evil cares, but simply the conflicting claims of home and business and money and pleasure that strangle spirituality and choke the Word of God. Writing to Timothy, Paul makes a passing reminiscence that illustrates man's apostasy in every generation, "For Demas hath forsaken me, having loved this present world." John in his First Epistle puts it quite categorically, "Do not love the world or the things of the world. If anyone loves the world, love for the Father is not in him." In Romans Paul compares Christians to strangers in a foreign country, living in a state of tension with language, customs, traditions and standards alien to their redeemed nature, and he admonishes them to resist the subtle pressure, "Do not be conformed to this world." "Religion that is pure and undefiled before God and the Father is this," writes James, "to visit orphans and widows in their affliction, and to keep oneself unstained from the world."

Louis Evans[1] tells of a man who entered the hut of a British officer in Africa, and saw his friend clad in a formal dinner jacket, sitting at a table, before him the appointments of a formal dinner. He said, "Man, are you going crazy? Dressing for dinner among a lot of African savages!" "No," replied the officer, "I dress for dinner once a week. I have to. I belong to the British Empire, and my customs and standards are not those of the Hottentots. There is no reason why I should live and act as they do. Furthermore, if I did not dress for dinner once a week, I should soon be living like the savages about me."

[1] Louis H. Evans, *Youth Seeks a Master* (Fleming H. Revell Company, New York 1951), p. 91

The true follower of Christ finds himself in exactly that position. He is like a gentleman set amid savagery, or as Reinhold Niebuhr calls him, "moral man in an immoral society." Through faith in Christ he has become a member of the redeemed community, but he still has to live and work and do his daily business in a world that is largely unredeemed. Someone has described it poetically as

> "this world
> Of coins and wires and motor horns, this world
> Of figures, and of men who trust in facts,
> This pitiable, hypocritic world
> Where men with blinkered eyes and hobbled feet
> Grope down a narrow gorge and call it life."[1]

The Christian must guard unceasingly against the peril of worldliness. It becomes a real problem for him simply to survive as a Christian and to resist the pressure of values, standards, loyalties and goals which are alien to his redeemed nature. Inevitably he must appear stuffy and priggish. Inevitably the Church, in order to preserve its identity, must retreat into what seems like a shell of otherworldliness.

Out of this situation, and as an answer to it, arose the whole development of monasticism in medieval Christianity. Convinced that they could neither resist the world nor change it, men renounced the world's cares and responsibilities, took the vows of poverty and celibacy, and isolated themselves into little "saved" groups apart from the sinful world. So far as they could see, the Church and the world sat at separate tables, and since the world was lost to the Devil anyway, the best thing the Church could do for the world was to withdraw from it and pray for it.

Even outside the Church of Rome the separatist principle survives today in certain ultra-conservative religious groups. A few years ago some communities in Eastern Canada protested against the intrusion of an extreme fundamentalist sect from the United States. And with good reason. These

[1] Hermann Hagedorn, *The Great Maze – The Heart of Youth* (The Macmillan Co., New York, 1916)

people are a social anachronism. They strip their farmhouses of modern conveniences, travel by horse and buggy, dress in the style of two hundred years ago and forbid their children to attend the local school. A Broadway musical called *Plain and Fancy* caricatured these people and made their quaint other-worldliness seem rather endearing, but we cannot believe that such extreme other-worldliness authentically represents the religion of the New Testament and especially the character of Christ himself. The Son of Man came eating and drinking. He graced a wedding feast. He mingled with publicans and sinners. To him the world was not an evil thing that one renounced before entering the Kingdom of God. Either one brought the world itself into the Kingdom, or one did not come at all.

More subtly, separatism survives in modern Christianity. Indeed one sees a strange paradox here. The Church of Rome, still erecting stone cloisters, seeks to dominate the world and to bring all areas of the common life—education, medicine, marriage, journalism, labour relations and politics —under its iron control. Protestantism, which does not erect stone cloisters, swings to the opposite extreme, and with its "hands off" policy erects a cloister of the mind more impenetrable than the walls of a medieval monastery. I am not referring here to what has been called "unethical evangelicalism", the spiritual snobbishness of pious little enclaves who do, in fact, boast, "To us God reveals and proclaims everything. He does not trouble himself with the rest of the world; we are the only beings with whom he has dealings." Our concern is with the principle of separation that pervades all Protestant thinking, our conviction that the Church and the world still sit at separate tables, a conviction so fanatical that ultimately it would divorce the world—politics, education and the rest—not only from the Church, but from the religion of Jesus Christ altogether.

On one occasion I bumped into a friend at a golf club and greeted him, "Hello, I haven't seen you around before." "Well," he explained, "I don't play much golf; just occasionally when I'm in the mood. But it's nice to belong to the club. I can come here to eat and drink and meet my friends

and generally take advantage of the place when I want it."
We said "good day" to each other, and it occurred to me
afterwards that he had voiced the attitude which many
people have toward the Church. They look upon the Church
as a religious club in which they "hold membership" and of
which they may or may not avail themselves as the whim
takes them. The minister is a combination "pro" and business manager; they pay him to keep things going, especially
during the off-season when they have more important things
to do. Like a golf club, a Church exists for their enjoyment,
a kind of retreat from the burdens and responsibilities of the
world. Just as they "get away from it all" on the fairways,
so they "get away from it all" in the Church.

It was Viscount Melbourne who, after reading a sermon
by G. W. E. Russell, made the famous remark, "Things have
come to a pretty pass when religion is allowed to invade the
sphere of private life." Whether he realizes it or not, the
average Christian suffers a spiritual schizophrenia, a divided
personality, like a man who resides in two separate cities,
maintaining two separate domiciles and supporting two
separate families. As a Christian he lives in the Church; as
an office-clerk, a teacher, an industrialist, a farmer or a
factory-worker, he lives in the world and, without any conscious hypocrisy, he sees no relationship between the two
except on the most superficial level. He becomes infuriated
when his church begins meddling in political and social
issues and when his preacher fails to stick to what he understands as the Gospel. Out in the world he will not even discuss his religion; piety he considers vulgar. He renders to
Caesar the things that are Caesar's, and to God the things
that are God's.

What happens as a result of this separation between the
Church and the world has been timelessly portrayed in the
Old Testament, in Jotham's famous Parable of the Trees.
The trees once decided to appoint a king. The choice of their
committee fell logically upon the olive tree, symbol of
royalty, source of the sacred oil used to anoint distinguished
personages. But the olive tree refused the honour, declaring
it of lesser importance than the business of producing olives.

Next the committee went to the fig tree, symbol of their economic structure, provider of staple food. But the fig tree calculated the financial loss involved and declined the nomination. Finally, they approached the vine, bearer of grapes and symbol of pleasure. But the vine only laughed and declared in effect, "Who in his right mind would exchange a distillery for a sceptre?" Whereupon the bramble, who had been quietly awaiting his chance, stepped forward and ingratiatingly suggested that with sufficient pressure he might be drafted for the kingship. "I'm not seeking it, mind you, but if you insist. . . ." By this time the trees were fed up with looking and in a mood to consider any available candidate. So the bramble, with nothing but thorns on it, incapable even of casting sufficient shadow for anyone to lie down in and protect himself from the burning heat of the sun, the worthless bramble, by default of worthier, more experienced candidates, became king of the trees.

This parable recalls the words of Edmund Burke, "All that is needed for the triumph of evil is that good men do nothing." One need not infer from it that all non-Christians who offer themselves for public service are dishonest or incompetent, but the lesson is inescapably clear; namely, that if we Christians make our religion a private affair and fail to accept its social implications, then the social initiative in the world where we have to live may be taken by unqualified, self-seeking men who create a situation inimical to the cause of Jesus Christ.

The world of politics is a veritable happy-hunting-ground for self-seekers. I once knew a man who sought election to his local Council for no other reason than to engineer with public tax money a new road into his tourist resort. He made no secret of this motive. Everybody knew it and everybody grumbled about it, but no one opposed him. He got elected by default. Even the leading laymen of the local churches could not see in this shameful situation a challenge to their Christian responsibility as citizens. They believed that they had done their duty by simply "sounding off" in self-righteous indignation. No doubt they rationalized their inertia by dismissing politics as a dirty business, no place for a refined and sensitive man. They forgot that the dirtiest, most corrupt place in all the world was a skull-shaped hill called Calvary.

William Ewart Gladstone was by nature a refined and sensitive man, a student of Greek culture, who never conquered his early desire to take holy orders in the Church. Though a politician by career, he hated politics and throughout his life yearned to retire and devote himself to the pursuits of the mind and spirit, yet he felt himself driven by Divine impulse to place his great gifts at the disposal of his country. Gladstone believed that in the service of God politics and religion are all of one piece and that if we keep politics out of religion, as we are often urged to do, we shall soon discover that we have kept religion out of politics and have built the City of Destruction instead of the City of God.

The world of culture is going more and more by default to the humanists. A few years ago the UNESCO *Courier* published a list of "the world's most translated authors for 1948–55". First in the list stood what? Not the Bible. Not Shakespeare. First stood the works of Lenin, of which nine hundred and sixty-eight translations were published during that period. Then came the Bible with eight hundred and eighty-seven. Third stood Stalin's writings with six hundred and eighty-nine. But here is the significant thing: none of the twenty-two American authors on the list wrote on politics, economics or religion, whereas nearly all the Communist authors wrote on politics and economics with a strong anti-religious bias. About the same time Bertrand Russell republished his collection of essays under the title, *Why I am not a Christian*, a book crammed with inaccuracies and unsupported generalities, yet a book which enjoyed a popular sale far in excess of any religious writing published in the same period.

Why should the spokesmen for our culture so invariably be the agnostics and the free-thinkers? Why should music and art and drama that exploit sordidness and disillusionment and boredom be taken as representing most authentically the spirit of our age? Why should cynical and godless intellectuals, who smile patronizingly from the television screen, be accepted as the authoritative interpreters of the human situation? Is it that men of faith have nothing to say, no word of hope or healing or judgment, or is it that Christian educators, Christian journalists, Christian poets and Christian artists have not the imagination or the courage to articulate their faith through media that men can understand? We place a high premium these days on freedom of thought and expression, but we forget that what is achieved is so often the freedom of a ship which has lost both anchor and rudder and consequently drifts, the victim of any wind that blows.

Consider the world of social reform. In his book, *Your Other Vocation*,[1] Elton Trueblood refers to the provinces of the later Roman Empire. These provinces retained the forms of Roman sovereignty but they were actually lost, and when the barbarians came, they fell almost without a struggle. Trueblood then points us to certain lost provinces of the Christian faith such as the labour movement. He reminds us that those who fought the battles of the working man a century ago were convinced Christians, men whose Christian compassion drove them into the arena of social reform. More often than not the Church, far from baptizing their crusade, aligned itself with the forces of reaction and consequently lost its greatest social opportunity.

How many trade union leaders today are active and vocal in the life of the Church? How many committed Christians, as an expression of the Christian obedience, deliberately seek positions of leadership in the labour movement? At an assembly of the Canadian Congress of Labour one of the delegates, himself a union leader and a devout Christian layman, scribbled a note and passed it to the chairman. He asked, "How can there be a closer relationship between organized labour and the Church?" He received his answer on the back of an old envelope. In effect it read, "Let the Church entertain the possibility that in some disputes organized labour may be right." Until the unions are controlled by Christians, there is always a danger that they will be controlled by Communists. As long as the Church exists like

[1] Harper and Brothers. (New York 1952)

a religious club content to serve a relatively privileged stratum of society, it will surrender the initiative in social reform to the barbarians.

Raphael's famous painting of the Transfiguration portrays the Church as it sometimes stands in relation to the world. It is a great picture, very tall. In the foreground, dark against the perspective of the Mount, we see the epileptic boy with twisted limbs and rolling eyes and slobbering lips, surrounded by the little group—the parents pleading, the apostles help-less, the scribes mocking. Then on the Mount high above stands the Lord of Glory, lifted from the earth, with Moses and Elijah beside him, and the three chosen disciples pros-trate in adoration. Perhaps Raphael, when he painted the picture, did not realize how ironically it symbolized the Church as the Church so often appears—an enclave of pious souls, smugly secure on their height of spirituality, who could not care less about the world beneath them, a world diseased, distracted and desperately in need of healing.

We take it for granted these days that the Church has lost popular support in Europe, but it was an American maga-zine of great sophistication that declared editorially during the war: "Christian leadership has passed from the hands of the Church to the hands of the active and practical laity—the statesmen and educators, the columnists and pundits, the scientists and great men of action. This is another way of saying that there is no true *Christian* leadership at all." Some of the Church's critics speak less kindly; they despise the Church for its other-worldly irrelevance. One of them caricatures the Church as an old-fashioned guest at a new-fashioned cocktail party; she is invited and treated politely, but everyone wonders why she dresses as she does, and why she comes at all when she understands so little of the con-versation.

What a ghastly misconception of Christianity which in actual truth should be the most worldly of all religions! Some great ethnic faiths—Islam, Buddhism, Hinduism—do despise the world and seek to escape from it, but Christianity loves the world and works actively for its redemption. "The Church," wrote John Henry Newman, "was framed for the express purpose of interfering (or, as irreligious men will say, meddling) with the world." Why? Because this world is God's House. God created the world, and his creation pleased him; "He saw that it was good." Moreover, God accepts responsibility for the world; he governs it, provides for it and reaches out to deal with it. When the world in its sin fell away from God, God in his grace entered the world, identified himself with its perishing condition and in the death of his Son upon the world's Cross acted to save the world. "God so loved the world that he gave his only begotten Son. . . ." We Christians are the recipients of God's love, not because we belong to the Church, but because we belong to the world, "this world of coins and wires and motor horns", which is not the Church and is sometimes against the Church. And because God loves the world he will have the world, if not through the Church as it now is, then through the Church as it will be when God himself has refined and renewed it.

". . . they dragged . . . some of the brethren before the city authorities, crying, 'These men who have turned the world upside down have come here also.'" Turning the world upside down—what a glorious crime to commit! And how true to the essential spirit of Christianity! The Lord of Glory ever entreats the Father for his disciples, "I do not pray that thou shouldst take them out of the world, but that thou shouldst keep them from the evil one." A cloister, yes, but not separated from the world; rather the world itself that cloister; the Christian life lived not outside the earthly struggle but within that struggle as a cleansing and leavening influence; Christ glorified, not by renouncing the world, but by bringing the world, the world of commerce and industry, education and entertainment, politics and social relations under the rule of his Kingdom.

16

AN IDEA WHOSE TIME HAS COME

"You shall be my witnesses in Jerusalem and in all Judea
and Samaria and to the end of the earth."

(Acts 1 : 8)

W E USUALLY have regard to the geographical nature
of our Lord's commission, and we invoke it to support the Church's responsibility for evangelism at
home and abroad. But look now at the men to whom the
Risen Lord entrusted this globe-circling assignment for the
extension of his Kingdom. There was Peter, a fish-merchant
from Galilee, and James and John engaged with their father
in the same trade. There was Matthew, a civil servant whom
Jesus had called from his place at the seat of custom. All of
the disciples had one thing in common: they earned their
living in what we call the secular vocations; not one was a
priest or a bishop or a rabbi or in any sense a religious professional; all of them were laymen.

Christianity began that way, as a laymen's movement,
its Founder a carpenter by trade and its greatest missionary
a tentmaker. Not to a conclave of clerics but to a loosely-
organized group of laymen Christ entrusted the issues of his
Kingdom. They were to be his witnesses, in Jerusalem and
in all Judea and Samaria and to the end of the earth. Like
a man who stands up in a courtroom and says, "Yes, I saw it
happen, and this is how it happened," so the disciples were
to go throughout the world witnessing to the saving facts
of Jesus Christ as they had experienced them.

The centuries brought a subtle change. As the Church
grew large and unwieldy, it required leadership by men who
no longer earned their living in secular vocations, but who
gave their full time to the tasks of oversight and supervision.

Within Christianity, as within all religions, there emerged the religious professional, the pastor, at first distinct from his brethren only by virtue of the function which he performed. Gradually, however, the pastor evolved into a priest, possessing authority and power, and elevated by his ordination to the status of mediator between God and man. The priest was a higher species of Christian, as much a professional in religion as the physician is a professional in medicine, or the mechanic a professional in repairing your motor-car. You needed a priest in order to be saved; he alone knew the formula of salvation, he could forgive your sins, he possessed the keys of the Kingdom of heaven. His life of celibate discipline and asceticism was considered the only true religious life, the only real Christian vocation or calling. The very word "Church" became different in its meaning; it no longer denoted the whole people of God, for though the laity came within the Church, they no more constituted the Church than a theatre audience constitutes the theatre. The Church, as such, had become identified with its ecclesiastical hierarchy, and its witness became the exclusive role of a cast of religious professionals. It was a far cry from those simple beginnings when a few fishermen started out in obedience to Christ to tell the world what they had seen and heard.

Victor Hugo declared that nothing is so powerful in this world as an idea whose time has come. The Protestant Reformation rediscovered an idea which for many centuries had been buried beneath the rock of ecclesiasticism: the idea that every Christian is a priest, not only in his right to approach God without a human mediator, but also in his responsibility to be a minister of the Gospel and a witness to his fellow-men. The reformers rediscovered this idea, but its time had not come even in their day. It remained dormant for four centuries, and only now has it found liberation in what Hendrik Kraemer calls the "Lay Renaissance", the most significant movement in modern Christianity. One of the most hopeful signs of the renewing activity of the Holy Spirit in the Church today is the rebirth of the New Testament idea of the Church, the awakening of laymen in all countries and in all communions to their membership in the whole people of God and their rôle in the total life of the Church. Just as the sixteenth century will be remembered for the Reformation, the eighteenth century for the Evangelical Revival, and the nineteenth century for the outreach of missions, so the twentieth century will go down in Church history as the Laymen's Century.

As a sign of this "lay renaissance" we can point to the Lay Institutes and Evangelical Academies throughout Europe, where mature laymen and laywomen come to study theology and then return to their daily work as housewives, farmers, teachers and clerks, with new insight into the ways in which their common tasks can facilitate the growth and application of the Gospel. No single event in the life of the Church attracts wider attention and achieves greater significance than the "Kirchentag" in West Germany, an annual conference which brings together half a million European laymen, as well as many visitors from overseas. Within Roman Catholicism the Christopher Movement exists to encourage the religious activity of all believers, each in his own calling; it is central to the Christopher or "Christ-bearer" idea that God has put "a little bit of the missionary" in every human being. The health and soundness of the Church in North America today can be traced not least of all to the vigour and virility of its lay activities. Every summer thousands of laymen in Canada and the United States attend conferences to study and discuss the practical ways in which their daily lives can be an effective witness to Christ, and many return to their homes and work with a new vision of their Christian vocation both within and beyond the bounds of the visible Church.

More important than the signs of the lay renaissance, however, is the principle behind it, this powerful idea whose time has come in our day. It is the realistic recognition that the tasks confronting the modern Church are too great and too serious to be undertaken by religious professionals alone. It is the recognition that while ministers remain the Church *within* the Church, laymen are the Church *out in the world*, and that if the Church is going to witness before the world in such a way as to make a Christian impact upon it, this will have to be through the lives and deeds of its laymen. Of all the reports presented at the Second Assembly of the World Council of Churches at Evanston, none has been more widely quoted than the report on the Laity. It said that "the real battles of the faith today are being fought in factories, shops, offices and farms, in political parties and government agencies, in countless homes, in the press, radio and television, in the relationship of nations". The report went on to say that while we hear very often that the Church should "go into these spheres", the fact is that the Church is already in these spheres in the persons of its laity. It is not enough to say that laymen *are* the Church; we must go a step further and recognize that laymen are the Church out in the world; they are *the Church's link with the world.*

Of course, it would be a disservice to the cause of Christ if the lay renaissance were to depreciate the Church's ordained ministry. In America no one has exploded more bombs under lazy laymen than has Elton Trueblood, the Quaker philosopher, but unfortunately, because of his Quaker background or in his zeal for positive ideas, he seems to hold a somewhat lower conception of the ministry than that held in most Christian traditions. In his writings he dwells monotonously on the "stigma" of being a religious professional. He says, "In many fields, such as natural science, the increased professionalism of the individual makes him more trustworthy, whereas in the life of religion the increased professionalism may make him less trustworthy". Trueblood believes that the layman can say essentially the same thing as the clergyman, but more effectively because he is not paid to say it, and with a certain "freshness". In other words, people take it for granted that ministers will be Christians and say pious things, but when a layman, a man who does not have to be a Christian, begins talking religion, they sit up and take notice.

True as that may be, it would be unfortunate if it discouraged young men from offering their lives to the full-time service of Christ in his Church. We all make foolish mistakes. One of mine was a sermon in which I said that a Christian engineer can serve Christ as sacrificially as a Christian minister. In the congregation that evening was a minister's son, a boy born to be a minister and possessing every quali-fication for the ministry, yet seeking everywhere an excuse for not entering the ministry. I gave him that excuse, but I was wrong. In terms of sacrifice, look at it this way. A Chris-tian engineer, if he loses his faith, can go on being an engineer, holding the same job, supporting his family and preserving his position in the community. A Christian minister, if he loses his faith or his voice or his health or his reputation, has lost everything. He has no other skills, no other means of earning a livelihood. He has given everything that a man can give to Christ. Interpret it how you may, something happens to a man when the Church lays hands on his head and or-dains him with the solemn words, "Take thou authority to preach the Word of God and administer the sacraments in the congregation." The Church's ministry is not a mere human arrangement arising from the fact that the Church, like every organization, must have officers and agents. The ministry is part of the Church's God-given equipment, necessary and indispensable. Every vocation can be a Christian vocation, but it is not without significance that in recent years increasing numbers of middle-aged men have given up lucrative business and professional careers, enrolled in theological colleges and sought ordination to the priest-hood and the ministry of the Word and Sacraments because they wanted Christ to have more of them than they could possibly give in their secular callings.

Nevertheless, in his opportunity to bear an effective wit-ness for Christ, the layman does possess a distinct advantage over the ordained minister. It is really not hard for a clergy-man to be a Christian. By reason of his sacred calling the clergyman leads a cloistered life, a life that protects him against many of the world's temptations, but a life that also denies him the privilege of witnessing most courageously for Christ. Society closes many of its doors to the religious pro-fessional. He may be tolerated, but he is not especially wel-come in a railway carriage or a factory or a labour meeting or a public-house, even though he may discard his clericals and disguise himself as a man of the world. Once people learn his identity they shut up like clams or move to another seat. Ministers play a vital rôle in the Church, but it is rather like the rôle of heavy artillery in a war; they provide support from behind the lines, but they rarely get into actual man to man combat. Clergy remain the Church within the Church; laymen are the Church out in the world. They are the Church's link with the world, the means of grace, the living channel through which the transforming power of God reaches into all areas of the common life.

This is the idea whose time has come—the awakening of laymen to their membership in the whole people of God and their rôle in the total life of the Church. Yet it would be naïve to suppose that the idea has caught on completely. The Church itself has a long way to go, as becomes evident from the composition of its official councils where bishops, theologians and clergymen, who comprise one per cent. of total church memberships, do all or most of the talking. The World Council of Churches may issue a report on the vocation of the laity, yet among the delegates appointed to attend the Assembly at New Delhi there are remarkably few who earn their living as laymen. Too often the Church gives the impression of a paid quartette attempting to render the glory and majesty of Handel's *Messiah*. One wonders how the Church hopes to speak intelligently and relevantly to the political, economic and social problems of human society except through the voices of its laymen. "The Church," says Henry Van Dusen, "has no right to speak on issues of the secular order except as its pronouncements are informed and determined by the wisdom and experience of Christian laymen with first-hand knowledge of the problems in all their baffling complexity, inter-relatedness and inescapable relativities." We can put it even more bluntly and say that a conclave of clerical executives and theologians by itself has no more right to issue statements on economic problems than a group of labour leaders has to issue statements on the Nicene Creed.

The Church still has to define what it means by a good Christian layman; we have not yet advanced beyond the idea that essentially he is a man who assists his minister and does a faithful piece of work around the church. A prominent surgeon sought an interview with his minister. This man was an elected official of the church, but it troubled him greatly that the demands of his profession hindered attendance at committee meetings and prevented him from fulfilling his duties as conscientiously as he wanted to fulfil them. Therefore he offered to resign. The minister felt humbled by the interview. With a shock it came home to him how lamentably the Church has failed in its approach to laymen. Instead of asking, "How can the laity do more for the Church?" we should be asking, "How can the Church do more for the laity to help them in *their* problems?" Here was a great servant of the Church, a devoutly religious man, utterly dedicated to the ministry of healing which he performed in the spirit of Christ, a surgeon who never entered the operating room without a prayer on his lips, a man of all men in the most strategic position to bear an effective Christian witness—here he was declaring his unworthiness to be an elected church official because the hour of committee meeting found him at the very task for which God had ordained and equipped him.

The churches will put the kiss of death on the lay renaissance if they simply exploit it, simply use it for the old, old motive—to claim a more general, convinced, effective lay participation in their own programmes, more faithful attendance at worship, more active service on church committees, more generous contributions to church budgets. This marvellous awakening of laymen to their Christian vocation will become nothing more than a piece of ecclesiastical machinery, an impediment to the Kingdom of God, if it merely produces a class of clerical amateurs attempting unsuccessfully to perform the functions of the ordained ministry. From a week-end conference of laymen a dentist returned home on fire for Jesus Christ. Bursting into his minister's study he exclaimed, "I have had a tremendous spiritual experience and I want to tell people about it. Will you let me speak from the pulpit next Sunday?" "Yes," replied the minister, "if you will admit me to your surgery on Monday morning and allow me to drill the first patient's tooth." Then he added more kindly, "Leave preaching and reading the Lessons to me. This is my work, and I am qualified to serve Christ through it, but I am not qualified to serve Christ through your work. You are a layman. Take advantage of that fact and do something original. Your job, if you seriously want to witness for Jesus Christ, is not to bring the world into the Church where you spend one hour a week, but to take the Church out into the world where you spend one hundred and sixty-seven hours a week."

No, it has not yet caught on, this idea whose time has come in our generation, but when it does catch on, there will be a renewal of life in the churches comparable in its impact to the Protestant Reformation and the Evangelical Revival. It will revolutionize the concept of a local congregation which in many places still resembles a theatre audience made up of critical spectators who believe that they have performed something meritorious by their mere presence at worship. Instead of being the sum total of Christian responsibility, Sunday worship will be seen as but the beginning of Christian responsibility. A community of Christians will come together on the Lord's Day, and one of their number, because he has been trained and set apart to interpret the Word of God, will brief his fellow-workers and help them to begin a new week in *their* ministry. They will share in the world's labour, sitting at desks, counting money, operating machines or disciplining little children, but always the real priority will be given to the fact that they are volunteers in a Christian army who have accepted the Lordship of Jesus Christ. They will say, as William Carey said, "I cobble shoes to earn my bread and butter, but my business is to serve God."

"Nothing is so powerful in this world as an idea whose time has come," and what gives it power is its outworking in the lives of human beings. More than twenty years ago I was a member of a Bible Class attending the funeral of our leader. We were a small company in the crowd that thronged the church that afternoon, because this good man had also been a secondary school teacher, and hundreds of old students flocked to pay him tribute. Words can never estimate the influence of his Christian character on the lives of succeeding generations, but we might express it this way: he was a minister of the Gospel; his Church—a scientific laboratory; his congregation—students of all backgrounds and faiths; his sermons—the way he taught, the little philosophies woven into his teaching, the God whom he revealed in the mineral and the butterfly; his pastoral work—students who came to him with their personal problems, knowing that they would receive sympathetic advice and practical help; his reward—three of us from that little Bible Class are ministers today, and hundreds of lives bear some relationship to Jesus Christ because they saw Christ revealed in the life of this gentle and good man.

A poet once wrote, "The common tasks are beautiful if we have eyes to see their shining ministry." I wonder how beautiful we should find the tasks of an orderly in a hospital for aged and incurably sick people. To the average person it would be exhausting work, thankless, drab and perhaps repulsive, just a job, an unpleasant necessity in the grim business of earning a living. One orderly, however, though a humble man with little formal education and few gifts of intellect, performs his tasks with surprising dignity and efficiency. He takes a genuine pride in his work and speaks of it as a vocation requiring special skills and aptitudes. He handles these crotchety old men with such poise and gentleness, scarcely pays attention to the work of his hands, but gets through routine tasks to his patients' personalities. He really cares for them. If one has to be moved to another hospital for surgery, this orderly will travel with him in the ambulance, even during his off-hours. If one is dying, the orderly will stay at his bedside. This young man—he is still comparatively young—represents security and friendship for many of these pathetic people who have no one in the world to love them. Their eyes light up when he comes into the room with his cheerful smile. It is he who makes tolerable their last days of loneliness and infirmity and pain. He is a Christian, this young orderly. He goes to church on his free Sundays, but if worship be defined as communion with the Spirit of Christ, then his whole life is an act of worship.

These are the kind of men to whom Jesus spoke when he said, "You shall be my witnesses in Jerusalem and in all Judea and Samaria and to the end of the earth." To these he bequeathed his own ministry; to these he entrusted the issues of his Kingdom upon earth. That was how he intended his redeeming work to be carried on—not only by religious professionals, and even less by conclaves of ecclesiastical power, but by ordinary men and women penetrating the world where they live and work as a cleansing, leavening, healing influence and quietly witnessing to the redeeming love of God in Christ. "The scene of their action," writes Henry Van Dusen, "is the shop, office, market, public forum, political party. The time of their action is five days a week, eight hours a day *plus*. Garbed in business suits or workmen's clothes, they are making the world's decisions by which the world's life is ordered and determined. Through them the Word of God is not simply vocally proclaimed; it is being *lived* in specific acts in the world. The Word of God is the *work* of God *in action*. It is the word of God again 'taking flesh and dwelling among us, full of grace and truth'."

17

COINCIDENCE OR PROVIDENCE?

"We know that in everything God works for good with those
who love him, who are called according to his purpose."
(Romans 8 : 28)

YOU RECALL the Authorized Translation: "All things
work together for good to them that love God." It is a
comforting thought. If we can believe it, if we can
stake our lives on the literal truth that every discord in life's
music will ultimately make for its greater harmony, then we
can put up cheerfully with any disappointment, any frustration, any suffering or loss. "All things work together for
good . . ."—heaven knows, we want to believe it; we have
quoted it in times of trouble and tried to convince ourselves
of its truth when the house of life has come crashing down at
our feet, but somehow this pious optimism which heartens
us in the ivory tower of religious faith does not authenticate
itself on the hard road of actual experience.

Look at the world about us. The year past has been a depressing record of confusion and violence on a world scale
as East and West continue to bark at each other like a pair
of paranoids in a mental hospital. The cold war, the horror
of nuclear weapons and the menace of Communist power,
make it impossible for us to contemplate the future with any
pride or complacency. No amount of pious optimism can
disguise the fact that we face a crisis unequalled in human
history. Oscar Wilde used to say that there was enough
suffering in any lane in London to prove that God cares
nothing for his world; lust and pain and sorrow and anxiety
and gruelling disappointment. Of every four babies born in
some parts of the world today, three will die of malnutrition
or be condemned to chronic ill-health for the remainder of

their lives. Forty million refugees wander the earth's surface; behind the Iron Curtain distinguished intellectuals, sensitive artists and courageous churchmen have their personalities pulverized under the heel of tyranny. In the light of these and other depressing facts would you say that all things work together for good even to them that love God?

To what extent does our own personal experience verify the Great Apostle's claim? Sometimes after a week's ministry when at least one person has told me that he expects to die of cancer, and another that her husband has become an alcoholic, and others that their marriage is breaking up—after such a week I have difficulty convincing myself that the evil things are actually good. Can I ever forget my first funeral? A young woman, numbed with grief and far beyond the reach of comforting platitudes, stood beside a tiny white coffin containing the body of her two-year-old child. It happened at their summer home; the little one had slipped away unnoticed from the house and ventured to the edge of the water. Exactly twelve months earlier the child's father, a medical research specialist, had been bitten in the laboratory by a poisonous rat, and died. Try telling this young woman, now widowed and childless, that all things work together for good to them that love God.

Look at Paul himself. We marvel at his audacity in making so extravagant a claim. His own trials and hardships must have weighed heavily on his soul, because he deliberately threw them in the face of one church on whose behalf he had laboured and sacrificed. Listen, as he writes to the Corinthians:

> "Five times I have received at the hands of the Jews the forty lashes, less one. Three times I have been beaten with rods; once I was stoned. Three times I have been shipwrecked; a night and a day I have been adrift at sea; on frequent journeys, in danger from rivers, danger from robbers, danger from my own people, danger in the city, danger in the wilderness, danger at sea, danger from false brethren; in toil and hardship, through many a sleepless night, in hunger and thirst, often without food, in cold and exposure. . . ."

Here was a man who had come into direct contact with life's ugliness. Pain, suffering, treachery, frustration—these had been his constant companions, and we could forgive Paul if he had expostulated cynically, "Nothing works out in this world, nothing makes sense, nothing hangs together; life is just an insoluble puzzle, and to live is to be the victim of capricious fate."

"All things work together for good to them that love God." Yes, we have tried hard to believe that truth and we have pretended to believe it even when we were not sure. Somehow it seems the Christian thing to say under disappointing circumstances. Indeed, what greater incentive to a righteous and holy life than the assurance that we have the universe on our side, the guarantee of a happy coincidence in the working of things which in the long run will turn to our favour? But life makes mockery of such naïve expectation. Happy coincidence obviously plays no part in God's sovereignty. All things in this world do not work together for good, and there is no use trying to say that they do.

Our pulses quicken, however, as we turn to the more accurate translation of Paul's insight in the Revised Standard Version. Not ". . . all things work together for good," but ". . . we know that in everything God works for good with those who love him". There is no change in the essential meaning; both versions emphasize God's effective help in all the circumstances of life. The new translation, however, makes that help seem personal rather than mechanical. It looks for God not in the realm of coincidence where God can never be found, but in the realm of Providence which is God's own realm. Paul never affirms here or anywhere else that the universe is so constituted that everything will automatically work out to the satisfaction of religious people. He does affirm that God co-operates in all things for good with those who love him, and there is a subtle difference. Evil does not cease to be evil, suffering does not cease to be suffering, and sorrow does not cease to be sorrow, but in the context of religious faith, evil, suffering and sorrow take on a new appearance, and instead of cursing them for the hurt they bring upon us now, we accept them, believing that in the alchemy of his Providence God will ultimately use them for our good.

Now that is what Paul would have us believe—that in all places, even the gloomier and more discouraging corners of life, God co-operates for good with those who love him. It is a daring insight, but one that we ought to explore if the Christian Faith is going to make any difference in the way we react to the rough treatment that life sometimes hands out to us. Well, what about Paul himself? With his respect for candour and intellectual honesty he would not ask us to believe so compelling a claim unless he had measured it, tested it and verified it in the hard school of first-hand experience. Speak for yourself, Paul. Stand before us and tell us why you believe that "in everything God works for good with those who love him".

"Very well," replies the Great Apostle, "I shall tell you. Let me begin with my conversion. As a Jewish rabbi, fanatical about my faith, I saw myself ordained of God to exterminate this new movement called Christianity, drown it in its own blood if necessary, and I organized attacks upon the Christians, breaking into their houses and dragging them out to beat them and sometimes stone them to death. Dark night settled upon my soul when I realized that in fighting the Christians I had been fighting God, crucifying his Son afresh. What hope could there be for me now, I, whose passions, whose consuming zeal, whose fanaticism had damned me to eternal perdition? Yet, the miracle of it all is that these things did not damn me to perdition. God, who in everything works for good with those who love him, took the very qualities which had been my undoing—my passions, my consuming zeal and my fanaticism—and he redeemed them, he directed them into new channels and used them for his own glory."

Paul continues, "My ministry corroborates my conviction that in all things God works for good with those who love him. How well I recall our second missionary journey when I wanted so very much to push north into the Province of Bithynia, but obstacles blocked our path—unscalable mountains, foodless wastes, wretched climate, unfriendly people.

Our progress seemed so utterly impeded that one night at Troas on the shores of the Aegean Sea, I sat down and wept, wondering if we had come to a dead end. Then suddenly I saw a vision—a man from across the sea who said, 'Come over to Macedonia and help us.' Macedonia! Think what that meant! Corinth . . . Athens . . . Rome . . . Spain . . . the whole continent of Europe. Up to that point I had never dreamed of such worlds to conquer for Christ. I realized then that while God himself may not have frustrated us, yet he was co-operating with us in our frustration and using it for the accomplishment of his own larger purpose.

"Let me tell you about the thorn in my flesh," continues Paul, "that vexatious physical handicap that kept me in constant pain and proved such an impediment to my missionary labours. Three times I besought God that it should leave me, not for my own sake but for the sake of the work to which he had called me. 'How can a crippled man go the way of the Cross?' I demanded of him. But God shook his head and he just said to me, 'My grace is sufficient for you, for my power is made perfect in weakness.' God did not answer my petition, but he did answer me; he did not make life easier, but he did give me strength equal to life's demands; he did not remove the nagging thorn in my flesh, but he did help me to live with the thorn and transform it into a means of grace; he did not change negative circumstances, but he did co-operate with me positively in those circumstances, so that, looking back on them now, I know that they were good.

"We began with my new birth," concludes Paul, "we should end with my final imprisonment. You wonder how I endured it. With such an active career behind me and so many hopes and plans yet to be realized, why did I not curse the cruel fate that put me in Roman chains? Had God planned my captivity? I did not believe so, but I did believe that God would somehow use my captivity, that because of it people would hear of Christ who never heard of him before, and that my example of Christian fortitude under affliction would be a source of strength to others. These things happened, and they were not all. Up to that point I had written many letters—Corinthians, Galatians, Thessalonians and the rest, but always on the run, always hurriedly with no time for patient reflection. Now I felt the Spirit of God impelling me to take advantage of these quiet days and to share with the Churches in Ephesus and Colossae and Philippi my mature and carefully worked-out thought on the Christian faith and life. Somehow I felt that if posterity preserved and cherished any of my letters, they would be the ones written from a prison cell."

Thus would Paul verify his claim that "in everything God works for good with those who love him". It is a tremendous truth of wide application, though not everyone is qualified to profit by it. Dr. Edward Wilson, who accompanied Scott's expedition to the Antarctic and who perished there, wrote in his diary, "This I know is God's own truth, that pain and troubles and trials and disappointments are one thing or another. To all who love God, they are tokens from him. To all who do not love God and who do not want to love him, they are merely a nuisance." It requires more than a built-in or developed strength of character to rise above bitterness and cynicism and to find a positive meaning in negative circumstances. According to Paul it requires a new relationship to God, a relationship which he describes by the word *Love*. "We know that in everything God works for good with those who *love* him."

We must not interpret Paul's word as a mere beating of the drum for piety. It does not seem reasonable that a righteous God should refuse to co-operate for good even with his disobedient children, but surely it is reasonable that a Father God, whose essential nature is Love, cannot co-operate with us except as we love him in return. We see this in our human relationships. An earthly father loves his son, guides him according to a wise purpose and stands by ready to help him weave everything, even failures and frustrations, into the fabric of that purpose. The father, however, cannot help his boy, cannot do anything for him unless the lad is willing to be loved and helped by his father. It was a part of growing up for all of us that one day we got ourselves into a big enough mess so that we recognized the superior wisdom of our parents. Having skipped over the side of the nest and spread our wings, we found that solo-flying is a great deal harder than it looks. Now for the first time we realized that what we had considered an irrational and painfully restrictive discipline was really the expression of a loving purpose for our lives, and with a new humility and a new appreciation we looked up to our parents, voluntarily sought their advice, and in so doing, put ourselves in a position where they could help us. That is what Paul means when he says that "in everything God works for good *with those who love him*".

Paul's claim takes us into the very heart of the Gospel. It speaks to us of the one great and abiding reality in the world of our experience—the loving purpose of God our Father for each one of us. Paul was convinced of that purpose because he had seen it revealed in Jesus Christ. He knew that in the same Jesus who went about doing good, who healed the sick and cleansed the lepers, who died on a cross and rose from the dead and came to him on the Damascus Road and transformed him—in this same Jesus, the great, eternal, loving heart that beats at the centre of the universe had revealed itself. When Paul writes about our love for God, he means not some state of emotion that we generate like heat within our hearts, but rather our calm and rational response to what God is and what he has done. Loving God means believing in the loving purpose of good for all of us which he has revealed in Jesus Christ. Paul is very sure that we can enter into that purpose and co-operate with it, and in so doing, rise to such a measure of mastery over life's circumstances that what has hitherto seemed evil actually turns to our own good and the good of all men. Out of the same conviction Robert Browning writes:

"Then welcome each rebuff
That turns earth's smoothness rough,
Each sting that bids nor sit nor stand but go!
Be our joys three-parts pain!
Strive, and hold cheap the strain;
Learn, nor account the pang; dare, never grudge the throe!"

In a missionary magazine last year I read the inspiring

story of Mary Verghese. Dr. Mary Verghese is an Indian girl who qualified as an orthopedic surgeon at Vellore Christian Medical College in 1951. Two years later an automobile accident crippled her for life. Doctors had to break the tragic news that not only would she never walk again, but that from her arms downwards she would never feel again and never move again; all she had left was her head and her two arms. Dr. Mary took the blow with hardly a word. She believed that Christ had a purpose for her life, and despite every warning to the contrary, she expressed the calm faith that Christ would bring her into full medical work again. She became interested in leprosy patients, because at that time a French surgeon had perfected a technique for grafting tendons and transforming the wasted stumps of lepers into something like hands and feet. At her own insistence Mary Verghese underwent three long operations which resulted in her being able to sit upright in a wheelchair. Then she began to specialize all over again. Today she is reckoned to be one of the most skilful surgeons in the East. In the operating room at Vellore you will find her doing hand reconstructions, foot reconstructions and face reconstructions, the kind of surgery that can be performed from a wheelchair. You will also see the new light that comes into the faces of her patients as they watch her moving among their beds, someone more paralysed than they will ever be, someone who is only partially alive, who will never be any better physically, yet whose shattered life has achieved triumphant meaning in her love for Jesus Christ.

"We know that in everything God works for good with those who love him, who are called according to his purpose." What does this mean except that faith and obedience to Jesus Christ is the great and crucial issue in our own personal lives and in the life of our world today? God has not willed the present crisis, much less caused it; we ourselves have brought it on by a flagrant repudiation of his laws. Nor can we believe that God, even in answer to our prayers, will dissolve the present crisis as sunlight causes the early morning fog to disappear. Panic, tension, Communism, missiles, hydrogen bombs, sputniks, hunger and revolution—these are the "things" of our mid-twentieth century. Evil they are and evil they remain, and not even God in his overruling providence can make them good. But God can bring good out of these things. He can turn our present plight into the shock treatment of destiny; he can make it a storm that scatters the dense fog of intellectual conceit and spiritual confusion which has caused our civilization to drift from one disaster to another. We have God's promise that he will work with us and co-operate with us insofar as we respond to the loving purpose which he has revealed in Jesus Christ. That means that the decisive factor in our modern world, that which we neglect at our peril, is the mission of the Christian Church. It means that the world's salvation is not in the hands of politicians, economists and scientific experts, but in the hearts and minds and wills of those who love and serve and obey the Lord Jesus Christ.

18

THE GUIDED LIFE

SOME TIME ago a magazine asked the renowned theologian, Karl Barth, for a statement of the tasks and problems to which he would address himself if, in the light of
his past experience, he were only now beginning his work
as a theological teacher. Professor Barth graciously declined,
saying that it had never been his method to work according
to set programmes. Rather, his thinking and writing and
speaking issued from living encounters with people, events
and conditions that spoke to him, engaged his interest and
compelled him to say something about them. Barth said that
he felt like a man in a boat which he must row and steer
diligently, but which swims in a stream that he does not
control. It glides along between new and often totally strange
shores, carrying him towards the goals set for him, goals
which he sees and chooses only as he approaches them. He
said, "As I see it now, my theological career has been a
'succession of present moments'."

In a few short sentences Barth has given us a description
of the Christian life, a life lived in harmony with the purpose
of God, and therefore a life which knows itself directed according to the purpose of God. The Christian life is a guided
life; its course is charted by forces which it does not control,
and though it preserves a freedom of choice, yet it moves
along the stream with a very definite impulse toward goals
and tasks and relationships which have been set for it. Whoever honestly tries to follow Christ will find himself guided by
the Spirit of Christ. We can do no better than consider
this mighty theme of Divine guidance in the light of one
man's personal experience. In the sixteenth chapter of Acts,
describing one of the missionary journeys of Paul, we have a

dramatic and specific instance of Divine guidance in the great Apostle's career:

> "And they went through the region of Phrygia and Galatia, having been forbidden by the Holy Spirit to speak the word in Asia. And when they had come opposite Mysia, they attempted to go into Bithynia, but the Spirit of Jesus did not allow them; so, passing by Mysia, they went down to Troas. And a vision appeared to Paul in the night: a man of Macedonia was standing beseeching him and saying, 'Come over to Macedonia and help us.'"

I

Notice, first, how naturally the writer of Acts attributes these circumstances to the activity of the Holy Spirit. We do not know the precise nature of the impediments and impulses that directed Paul's labours, but had we been writing his biography we should no doubt have come up with some very human explanations. Forbidden to speak the word in Asia? The early Christians were forbidden under penalty of death to speak the Word in many parts of the Mediterranean world. Not allowed to go into Bithynia? At certain times of the year treacherous conditions prevented any traveller from moving in a northerly direction. A dream about a man from Macedonia? Assuredly Paul had dreamed many times of the possibility of extending his missionary journeys across the Aegean Sea into Greece. Thus *we* should have explained these circumstances of Paul's career. Not the writer of Acts, however; to him there was nothing fortuitous, nothing coincidental about them; he saw them as part of a Divine strategy; he believed that they came to Paul as the unmistakable guidance of God's Holy Spirit.

It would never have occurred to Paul himself not to believe in Divine guidance. We ask the very academic question, and we ask it as though somehow the issue depended upon our assent, "Does God guide? Has he a plan for the individual life, a plan which he communicates to the mind sensitized by prayer?" That question would have no reality for Paul. As a devout Jew, steeped in the Scriptures of the Old Testament, he would certainly believe in a personal God, actively interested in and dealing with his creation, a God so great that there can be no creature in his universe of whom he is not perpetually cognizant and conscious. As a Christian, Paul would believe in God as Jesus revealed him, a Heavenly Father who fashioned his children for a wise and good purpose, and who, while he respects the freedom of his children, continually reaches out to direct them along the paths of that purpose. Not for a moment would Paul explain the closing and opening of doors as mere human frustrations and opportunities; he would simply assume that the Spirit of God was guiding him in those directions and to those areas where his work would have the most enduring results.

Did not our Lord make a promise of that kind to his disciples in the Upper Room? For three years he had been their Teacher, their Counsellor in the things of God, and with him at their side to guide and direct them, they felt capable of living in harmony with the will of God. But now he was to be taken from them, so how would they ever know what to do, where to go, how to serve? Five times, as he comforts his sorrowing disciples, our Master makes the same gracious promise. He will not leave them as a flock untended, but will pray the Father who will give them another Counsellor to be with them forever, even the Spirit of Truth. The Counsellor, the Holy Spirit, whom the Father will send in Christ's name, will teach the disciples all things and will bring to their remembrance all that he has said to them. The Counsellor, who proceeds from the Father, will bear witness to Christ. It is to the advantage of the disciples that the Master go away, because if he does not go away, the Counsellor will not come to them, but if he goes, he will send the Counsellor. When the Counsellor, the Spirit of Truth, comes, he will guide the disciples into all the truth, for he will take what is Christ's, he will take the will and purpose of Christ for their lives, and declare it to them.

Whoever seriously tries to follow Christ can be certain of the Spirit of Christ to guide him along the paths that he must take. At a conference of the Church, seven young men, about to be ordained to the Christian ministry, gave their personal testimonies. With one accord they spoke of a more-than-human impulse which directed and fairly drove them into the full-time service of Christ in his Church. One of them had been a toolmaker, a labour union leader with six hundred men under his control. "It made me arrogant and egotistical," he said, "to know that I wielded such power over these men in relationship to their jobs. The one thing I had no power to do, however, was to help my men in their personal lives. They came to me with their problems, their loneliness, their fears, and it was that more than anything else that drove me to a new study of the Christian Faith and eventually into the ministry. I did not want to be a minister. I came in under the lash. But I have discovered that when God wants something of a man, he has persuasive methods of making his will known."

II

Notice also how unquestioningly Paul and his companions obeyed the guidance of God. If they did not doubt that the Spirit of Christ directs the servant of Christ, neither did they doubt that the servant should follow the Spirit's direction. Not for a moment did it occur to them that, having been denied entry into Asia and Bithynia, they should muscle their way into these countries and preach the Word of God in spite of obstructions. Nor did they question the reality or the validity of Paul's dream about a man from Greece who said, "Come over to Macedonia and help us." They could have mustered impressive arguments against preaching the Gospel in Europe before it had taken root in Asia, they could advance all kinds of reasons for confining their work to peoples and cultures of which they had some understanding, but they were men under authority. They believed that they could see what their Lord wanted them to do and they had no choice but to obey.

There is no use getting started on a purely theoretical discussion of Divine guidance. The subject cannot be discussed academically, and the unspiritual man is no more an authority on it than a religious celibate is an authority on married love. The guidance of God has to be experienced; it has to come clearly and unmistakably in some vital issue of your life. The most important thing we can say about Divine guidance is this: it comes only if you intend from the very first to obey it. It is guidance that God gives to us, not advice. A fine Christian girl falls in love with a splendid young man who does not share her religious faith. Should she accept his proposal of marriage? "I have prayed about it for weeks," she complains, "I have tried to find out God's plan for my life, but he does not answer." Well then, you had better learn the truth, young lady. God is not mocked. He knows that you will finally do what you want to do regardless of his purposes; he knows that your heart and not your soul will dictate the decision. It is foolish to suppose that he will guide you.

Looking at a human parallel, let us suppose that the years have endowed you with a wisdom and a sympathy which your friends respect. One day there comes to you a younger colleague who confides a problem of his personal life and frankly asks for your advice. Modestly you decline to advise him; your judgment may be sound, but you hesitate to play God. Still he persists. "I am serious," he says, "I want you to tell me the best thing to do in this situation." It is a delicate matter, but you agree to think about it for a while and make a few inquiries. At last you get in touch with your friend and say to him, "In the light of all the facts I suggest that you do such and such." "How unfortunate," he replies, "because I have reached an altogether different decision. In fact I had already decided when I spoke to you, but I thought it might be interesting to see if your viewpoint confirmed my own!" Surely you would feel foolish and inclined to say "Never again!" when people ask for your advice.

We can phrase this truth in the form of an admonition: never pray for the guidance of God unless you seriously intend to follow it. Otherwise that guidance will not come, the heavens will be as brass, and you will get nothing for your prayers but a pair of sore knees. The essential condition of all effectual prayer is sincerity, and that means an open

mind, a receptive heart and a will that can be changed and
moulded to the will of God. Such prayer may have startling
results, because so often the finger of God points in a direction other than that which we ourselves might choose. For
Paul it pointed across the ocean, for Abraham to the
unknown, for Albert Schweitzer to Africa, and for Jesus to
a Cross. Sometimes the guidance of God contradicts every
human consideration of commonsense and caution, and one
has no motive for following it save that of obedience to God.
Without the intention of that obedience, however, there
will be no disclosure of the Divine purpose. God guides only
the man who is prepared to obey him.

III

Notice, however, that Paul and his companions still had
to weigh the human alternatives. Confident as they were of
directives from on high, it did not exempt them from the
necessity of making a rational decision. They knew that their
goals had been set for them and that if they obeyed the
guiding impulse of the Holy Spirit they must continue travelling west instead of remaining in Asia or pushing northward
into Bithynia, but they still had to choose these goals as they
approached them. The Spirit of God impelled them, but he
did not take them by the scruff of the neck. Nor did God
force them to answer the urgent appeal of the man from
Macedonia. Unquestionably God wanted them to preach
the Gospel in Greece; they knew that and they obeyed, but
they still had to make up their minds to obey.

How does the guidance of God make itself known? We
can only say that it comes to different people in different
ways. When the American journalist, Norman Cousins,
visited Albert Schweitzer in his jungle hospital at Lambaréné, he asked the great doctor whether he had decided
to give up his earlier careers in music and theology and become a medical missionary in response to direct Divine
guidance. Cousins says that he could not be sure whether
he had asked the most obvious question in the world, or
whether he was pushing at a door that was meant to be kept

closed. Dr. Schweitzer replied very simply that the pursuit of the Christian ideal was a worthwhile aim for any man. Then, after a moment, he added that he did not want anyone to believe that what he had done was the result of hearing the voice of God or anything like that. The decision he had made was a completely rational one, consistent with everything else in his own life. Indeed, he said, some theologians had told him that they had a direct word from God. He did not argue. All he could say about that was that their ears were sharper than his. He said, however, that he believed in the evolution of human spirituality, and that the higher this development in the individual, the greater his awareness of God. Therefore if by the expression, "hearing the voice of God," one means a pure and lively and advanced development of spirituality, then the expression was correct. This is what is meant by the "dictates of the Spirit".[1]

We must not put the prayer for Divine guidance in a class with horoscopes, ouija boards and automatic fortune-tellers. Many people, when they have prayed, make the mistake of settling back and expecting God to do the thinking for them. They wait for some supernatural sign, some inner voice that will release them from the necessity of making a rational decision. It does not happen that way, though, because even when we have sought direction from on high, we must still apply our own reasoning powers, believing that God's Spirit operates through those powers and that when the time for actual decision arrives, then and not before then shall we decide in accordance with God's will. The Holy Spirit does not supersede our intelligence, else why did God give us our intelligence? But the Holy Spirit sensitizes our intelligence to the will of Christ in any situation. Here is the most remarkable truth about our great theme—that only in retrospect do we become fully aware that the hand of God has been upon us. Only when we have prayed about something and then followed our best judgment and taken the leap of faith can we look back and be certain that the Spirit of God has been guiding us all along.

[1] Norman Cousins, *Dr. Schweitzer of Lambaréné* (Harper and Brothers, Publishers, New York 1960), p. 192

Suppose you have to deal with the unpleasant case of a dishonest employee. As a Christian you want to do what is both just and charitable, and quite humbly you say to God, "Lord, what wilt thou have me to do?" You postpone the issue until the last possible minute, hoping that the way will be made unavoidably clear, but you have nothing to go by except a growing conviction that, hazardous as it may be, your Christian duty lies in a certain direction. At last you take the leap of faith; for better or worse you follow the dictates of your own conscience; and suddenly there floods through your soul the most astonishing serenity and exhilaration, as though a crushing load had been lifted from your shoulders. Instinctively you know that you have done the right thing. You still had to weigh the human alternatives, still apply your own powers of reasoning, but you realize now that the Spirit of God was operating through those powers of reasoning, taking the things of Christ and making them known to you.

IV

Notice further that in Paul's life the guidance of God vindicated itself. The writer of Acts records only the barest details of Paul's missionary journey, but had he written as a typical biographer he would surely have described the apostle's feeling of disappointment at finding his way into certain countries blocked. No busy man appreciates having to deviate from his own preconceived plans, and undoubtedly Paul chafed with frustration at being forced to by-pass these Asiatic cities which were so important culturally and economically. However, Paul did not know at the time, no man alive could have known, that the centre of the world's life was soon to move westward; that Europe, not Asia, was about to become the commercial and colonizing centre of the world. Paul did not demand that kind of knowledge as a condition of his obedience. He obeyed in faith, even though he could not see that from little churches planted in Philippi, Thessalonica, Colossae and Corinth would spread branches of Christian influence soon to yield the rich fruit of Western civilization.

The Christian life reaches its supreme testing-point when a man has prayed for Divine guidance, and the finger of God points in a direction exactly opposite from the direction that he would choose for himself. Thomas à Kempis gave thanks to God in these sublime words, "Thou hast broken my dreams, but only that I might learn to think in thy broad day. Thou hast put aside my plans, but only that I might open my eyes to see the depth and clearness of thy plan for me." One does not give thanks in the valley of decision, however. It can be an agonizing experience to find that in some issue of immense personal significance your own will conflicts with the will of God; the things you want for yourself are not the things that God wants for you. Nothing can be more shattering than to plan your own future and to see your plans coming to fruition, only to hear the unmistakable voice of God saying, "Set these aside; I have other plans for you." Everything in you rebels; and like Moses in Midian and Jeremiah in Anathoth and Jonah on his ship bound for Spain, you argue with God, you tell him he must be mistaken, you try to run away from what God has clearly revealed to be his purpose for your life. Yet all the time you know that God is right and that, having sought his guidance and received it, either you must obey him now, or you can never ask for his guidance again.

We have to trust God, that is all. We have to believe that God is indeed the heavenly Father that Jesus portrayed him to be, caring for each of his children with an infinite and tender concern. Jesus pointed to human parenthood at its best and he said, "If ye, then, being evil, know how to give good gifts unto your children, how much more shall your Father in Heaven give the Holy Spirit to them that ask him?" Earthly children always have difficulty believing, as a popular television programme sets out to prove, that "Father Knows Best". But father does, in fact, know best. He has lived longer than his children, he has travelled the same road before them, he sees life from the larger perspective of maturity. He may seem old-fashioned, but he knows many of the angles and the answers. The point is that God, with his infinitely superior wisdom and knowledge, can see what we cannot see—the outcome of our decisions, the consequence tomorrow of what we decide today; and we can follow his plan for our lives knowing that, however strange and uncertain it may seem to us now, one day it will be vindicated.

As a young man Abraham Lincoln went to the Black Hawk War a captain and, through no fault of his own, returned a private. That brought to an end his military career. Then his little shop in a country village "winked out", as he used to say, marking his failure as a businessman. As a lawyer in Springfield, Illinois, he was too impractical, too unpolished, too temperamental to be a success. Turning to politics, he was defeated in his first campaign for the Legislature, defeated in his first attempt to be nominated for Congress, defeated in his application to be Commissioner of the General Land Office, defeated in the Senatorial Election of 1854, defeated in his aspirations for the Vice-Presidency in 1856, defeated again in the Senatorial Election of 1858. Yet 1861, exactly one hundred years ago, found him in the White House as President of the United States. And how did Lincoln interpret this strange succession of failures and frustrations which finally culminated in terrific personal victory? He said, "That the Almighty directly intervenes in human affairs is one of the plainest statements in the Bible. I have had so many evidences of his direction, so many instances when I have been controlled by some other Power than my own will, that I have no doubt but what this Power comes from above."

The supreme truth to remember when God's will conflicts with our own is that God knows what is good for us better than we know it ourselves. His purpose may seem strange and unwelcome to us now, but we can be absolutely certain that it will be vindicated. Let us never make the mistake of judging God's over-all plan for our lives by that portion of it which he happens to reveal today. God has all eternity in which to bring his plans to fulfilment, and God's purpose will unfold in his way and his time, not ours. Our Lord Jesus in the Garden of Gethsemane resisted the guidance of God. "O my Father, if it be possible, let this cup pass from me. . . ." Even to the mind of the Master, perfectly attuned as it was to the mind of his Father, the Cross must have seemed the most futile, most disastrous event in the history of the world. Yet out of the defeat of the Cross God brought victory, out of its weakness he brought strength, out of its death he brought life. Man's obedience is the key that unlocks the power of God. God gives victory, strength and life to every man who, having prayed for his guidance and received it, can then say, "Not my will but thine be done."

19

DRIFTING AWAY FROM REALITY

"Therefore we must pay the closer attention to what we have heard, lest we drift away from it. For if the message declared by angels was valid and every transgression or disobedience received a just retribution, how shall we escape if we neglect such a great salvation? It was declared at first by the Lord, and it was attested to us by those who heard him, while God also bore witness by signs and wonders and various miracles and by gifts of the Holy Spirit distributed according to his own will."

(Hebrews 2 : 1–4)

IN THE Canadian School of Missions at Toronto there hangs a pair of portraits painted in 1903 and 1904 by Dr. J. W. L. Forster. They symbolize the spiritual biography of a certain Miss Smart, a young art student whom Dr. Forster used as a model. Miss Smart travelled extensively at one period of her life, especially through India where she came so strongly under the influence of Eastern philosophy and mysticism that she lost her grip on the realities of the Christian Faith. The first painting, bearing the title "Perplexed", shows her in this spiritually vacuous condition. She is gaudily dressed in colours of green, red and gold and surrounded by a number of pagan symbols, including a crystal gazer's ball. She appears dejected and disillusioned like one who has wandered into a maze of artificiality and who desperately longs to find her way back to the eternally real.

It could be a picture of every man's spiritual biography. It is wrong to suppose that we can possess our religion as we possess a piece of furniture and that once we have laid hold upon the Christian Faith, nothing can wrench it from our grasp. What happened to that young art student can

N

happen to any one of us. The seed may have been well sown in our childhood and youth, but, as Jesus made clear in his parable, the cares of this world, the delight in riches and the desire for other things may so smother the Word of God in our lives that it becomes lost under a tangled mass of weeds and thorns.

About the year 80, at a time when it was not easy to confess the name of Christ, an unknown Christian of great intellectual genius wrote a letter to a little Church in Rome. This letter has been preserved in the New Testament: we call it *The Epistle to the Hebrews*. Interspersed among its profound theological dissertations on the person and work of Christ, we find some practical, down-to-earth Christian counsel, obviously written by a minister worried about his people because he is separated from them and because he knows the difficulties and dangers that they face. He fears that some of them, removed from his influence and pressured by pagan society, may be falling away from the essentials of the Christian faith, and he admonishes them in language they can understand. "Therefore we must pay the closer attention to what we have heard, lest we drift away from it." The picture is that of a ship which has been carelessly allowed to slip away from the harbour and which drifts to destruction because the pilot has been asleep at the helm and has forgotten to allow for the wind or the current or the tide.

Society is filled with decent, self-respecting people whose lives were once moored to the great Christian certainties but are now dangerously adrift on the high seas of indifference and materialism. Not that they ever deliberately turned their backs on God and repudiated their Christian convictions; their falling away was more unconscious and subtle. Like G. K. Chesterton in his early years, they put their religious beliefs in a drawer, and when they went to look for them again, they found the drawer empty. Even now some of us may feel ourselves drifting away from the realities of salvation. We have not yet lost sight of these realities, but we feel them slipping from our grasp as the problems of life and the world perplex our minds and trouble our hearts. To us the admonition of the New Testament comes with peculiar force and speaks as an authentic Word of God to our condition. William Barclay translates it thus: "Therefore we must the more eagerly anchor our lives to the things we have been taught, lest the ship of life drift past the harbour and be wrecked." To forestall this peril of the drifting life we must throw out the anchors of the soul, those great Christian certainties that will secure our faith against wind, current and tide. The author of Hebrews tells us that we have four such anchors.

I

First, the Divine origin of our Faith. "It was declared at first by the Lord. . . ." We cannot remind ourselves often enough that whereas some of the great world religions had their birth in the experience of men, Christianity arose out of an objective historical situation. Buddhism began with Gautama and the profound truths which he perceived under the Bo-tree; Islam started with Muhammad and the vision that came to him in a dream; Communism, and it resembles at least a parody of religion, began with Karl Marx writing furiously in the British Museum; but we have no record of any mystic or prophet or reformer sitting down and saying, "Go to now, I will invent a new religion and call it Christianity!" Even should we reverently call Jesus the Founder of our Faith, we are reminded that on the day of His crucifixion there was not another Christian left in the whole world. Christ is not the founder but the Foundation of Christianity. It is Christ we worship, not his teachings or his ideas, but Christ himself, because we believe that in him the Almighty God has entered our world and acted conclusively for our salvation.

Some years ago I attended a conference of intellectuals—as an observer, you understand—who were discussing the topic, "The Predicament of Modern Man". A distinguished professor of psychiatry argued strongly that we shall never resolve our human predicaments until we break loose from the inhibitions and superstitions of religion. He said, "It is time we recognized that we have within ourselves the power to create a better life and that our idea of God is nothing but a projection on the cosmos of our infantile father image." He received a reply from a Christian layman, also an intellectual—and here I express surprise at the popular illusion that to be an "egghead" a man has also to be an agnostic. This man replied to the psychiatrist, "We cling to the Christian Faith, as men have always done, not because we seek something outside ourselves, but because Something outside ourselves has sought us and laid hold upon us. It is not we but God who has taken the initiative."

We hear a great deal these days about the war of ideologies. At least one group in Western society publishes pamphlets to warn us that we shall not meet the challenge of Communism unless we define our Christian ideology more clearly and promote it with stronger passion. That might be sound strategy, except that Christianity is not and never has been a set of ideas. Christianity is a Gospel, the good news of an historic event which has radically and decisively altered the situation of man on this earth, and unless we Christians anchor our Faith to that historic certainty, we shall be forever adrift on the ocean of other men's ideas. We shall be like the hero, John, in C. S. Lewis's satire, *The Pilgrim's Regress*, tossed from one human philosophy to another, always searching, never finding, always travelling, never arriving, mocked by illusions and never closer to our island in the sea.

The ancient Greeks believed that somewhere there is a real world of which this world is only a kind of pale shadow, an imperfect copy, and that therefore the supreme task of life is to get away from the shadows and the imperfections and to reach reality. But this, declares the author of Hebrews, is exactly what Christ enables us to do. Christ brings us into touch with reality; indeed Christ *is* Reality, because in Jesus Christ the God who is eternally real has invaded our world and declared himself to be our Saviour.

II

The author of Hebrews holds up another anchor of the Faith, "It was attested to us by those who heard him." I hesitate to refer to Bertrand Russell's book, *Why I am not a Christian,* and thus attach to that collection of anachronisms and inaccuracies greater importance than it deserves. It is the typical diatribe of a man pre-eminent in his own sphere, but quite juvenile in another, writing about religion in happy ignorance of what present-day theologians are saying, and lampooning a concept of the Church which may have been valid in his remote boyhood, but is certainly not valid today. Consider this one categorical statement: "Historically it is quite doubtful whether Christ ever existed at all, and if he did, we do not know anything about him." I presume that Lord Russell expects to be taken seriously, in which case we must either pity the New Testament writers as the victims of an illusion, or else accuse them of wilfully conspiring to perpetrate the most colossal hoax in history.

Let us reduce our case to the simplest terms. Take any historical event, the Battle of Britain, for example. Richard Collier writes of his own terrific book, *The City that Would not Die,* that it is not the whole story, for that is beyond one man's power to tell. He says that no mortal man will ever know the full truth of what happened on the incredible night—May 10, 1941—when London burned. Such a night was not the best climate for pinning down matters such as what happened when. Most people were too frightened, too angry, too stunned, or too busy. Collier could as easily be writing about the crucifixion of Christ, that most terrible and cataclysmic event in history when darkness descended on the earth and lightning tore open the sky and the solid rocks convulsed and the minds of men were thrown into confusion and turmoil. No mortal man will ever know the full truth of what happened in that incredible period when God walked this earth in human form, yet who in his right mind would deny that the Christ-event took place, any more than he would deny that the Battle of Britain took place? Something happened in Palestine about the year A.D. 30, something that inspired the writing of Gospels and Epistles, that released latent spiritual powers in increasing numbers of human lives, that started the Church on its journey through the centuries, that turned the world upside down and changed the course of history. Generations from now, when full allowance has been made for disparity of detail and difference of interpretation, men and women will still be anchored to Christ by the written witness of those who heard him, who were so close to him, so involved in him, that their witness becomes a part of Christ himself.

When I feel myself losing hold on the verities of the Faith, I do not seek assurance from the agnostics or even from the theologians; I go back to the one place where a man can find certitude. I listen with Matthew to the Sermon on the Mount, I sit with Peter in the Upper Room, I kneel with John before the Cross, I stand with Mary outside the Empty Tomb, I ride with Paul on the Road to Damascus. I open the Testament and study the first-hand witness of those who heard him, and it anchors me to reality.

III

The author of Hebrews throws out another anchor when he says that "God also bore witness by signs and wonders and various miracles. . . ." In this scientifically-minded age we have an innate scepticism toward miracles and a natural aversion toward the religion that predicates itself on the miraculous. When the World Council of Churches convened at Evanston in 1954, the Religious Research Foundation of America set up a display in a glass case in the lobby of one of the hotels. It consisted of two pie plates, one filled with barren earth and the other with a tiny garden. Seeds had been planted in both plates and both had been carefully watered, but it seems that a group of people had prayed that one set of seeds would germinate and the other die, and their prayer experiment having proved successful, they now brought it to the attention of the Church. You can imagine how the World Council delegates reacted to this primitive voodooism which would insult the Almighty with petitions unrelated to human need. As one was overheard to say, "This sort of thing makes me sick!"

One thing about Jesus that should appeal to this scientifically-minded generation is the way that he sought *not* to commend himself by signs and wonders. He wanted men to believe in him for his own sake, for what he was and for what he taught them. On the very threshold of his ministry he renounced miracle-mongering as an enticement of the devil; consistently he refused to give the Pharisees a "sign" from heaven; once in a parable he said that "if men do not hear Moses and the prophets, neither will they be convinced if someone should rise from the dead". Christianity never moves from miracle towards faith, but always from faith towards miracle. We do not believe that Jesus was the Son of God because he rose from the dead; rather we believe that he rose from the dead because he was the Son of God. Miracles do not create faith, but miracles undergird faith; they "lift our drooping hands and strengthen our weak knees"; they keep us anchored to reality.

Since that very night when God came to earth as a baby in a barn, God himself has borne witness to his own revelation by "signs and wonders and various miracles". That Christianity should have survived at all, that it endured the bloody persecution of the first three centuries; that the Church in history should have been consistently reborn when everything in its own life and in the life of the world pointed to its approaching death; that in every generation enemies of Christ should turn to serve him and become his most fearless apostles; that men should love one another when they have every cause for hatred; that people should still pray in the name of Christ and find in their despair a new source of courage and hope, and that prayers should be answered, sometimes in ways beyond our wildest imagining—these are the miracles of the Faith, the signs and wonders that keep us from falling away. The factors that comprise any situation add up to a certain total, but the story of the centuries has been that where Christ enters a situation, the total is changed and a whole new dimension brought into human experience.

There is still no miracle more marvellous than that of a redeemed personality. The real miracles at the Evanston Assembly of the World Council of Churches were not in glass cases. At least one of them walked about on two legs—

a frail, yellow-skinned, be-spectacled little man from Japan named Toyohiko Kagawa. We all admired the greatness of this world Christian leader, his Christlike character, his immense spiritual power, the range of his influence and the extent of his witness. Yet the story of Kagawa's early years is an open book for all men to read. He was born in the slums, the child of a temporary infatuation, his father a typical example of the military caste of the nation, his mother a dancing girl, both Buddhists. Since his own mother would have nothing to do with him, he fell into the hands of his father's legal wife who resented him and bullied him and for eleven years made him a household slave. By all the laws of heredity and environment Kagawa should have grown up to be a mixture of brutality and libertinism, but somewhere along the way he met Christ, and a miracle took place, and life for him became an adventure in comradeship with the redeeming Son of God. I look at men like Kagawa, men who by the grace of God have been changed, born again, and they become my anchor as I begin drifting away from reality.

IV

One more anchor: "God bore witness . . . by gifts of the Holy Spirit distributed according to his own will." That is a tremendous scene in the opening chapter of the Book of Acts where the disciples meet with their risen Lord for the last time upon this earth. Eagerly they ask, "Lord, will you at this time restore the Kingdom to Israel—now that you have conquered the forces of sin and death and hell?" And Jesus replies, "No, my children. The Kingdom of God cannot be imposed on men from above, but only by one human being persuading another. You shall be my witnesses. You shall go throughout the world telling men about me—but not on the strength of your own resources alone. You shall receive power when the Holy Spirit has come upon you." The amazing thing about Christianity is not what men have been able to do for God, but what God, by the power of his Holy Spirit, has been able to do with men and through them when they have yielded their lives to him in obedience and surrender.

I once heard it said flatteringly to a successful minister that he might have succeeded in any one of a number of callings. With marvellous humility he replied, "You are wrong. My gifts are spiritual gifts. (He called them "charismatic" gifts.) God gave them to me for use within his Church. I should not possess them otherwise." How often Paul in his letters enumerates the spiritual gifts. As he sees it, every genuine service that we can render to the Church, every Christlike quality of character comes to us as a gift of the Spirit: "The fruit of the Spirit is love, joy, peace, patience, kindness, goodness, faithfulness, gentleness, self-control. . . ." We see these qualities in the lives of good men, writes the author of Hebrews, and like an anchor they hold us to reality.

There has never been a stronger argument for the Christian Faith than the example of one dedicated Christian. You may disagree with other people's ideas, you may punch holes in everything they believe about religion, but unless you have a mind as narrow as the neck of a bottle, the quality of their lives can scarcely fail to attract you. Louis Evans,[1] an American Church leader, tells of visiting a mission field in Korea and spending some time with the missionary doctor, a man who in answer to Christ's call had relinquished a lucrative practice at home. One day he said to Evans, "Would you like to see a major operation?" Evans replied that he would, and minutes later he stood in the operating room balcony along with a number of Korean medical students. The operation took seven hours. Several times he found the intense heat and ether fumes so overbearing that he had to leave the room to refresh himself. "Is every day like this?" he asked the surgeon when it was over. The surgeon only smiled. Beads of perspiration stood out on his forehead, his lips were purple with the strain, his hands trembled from fatigue. "Doctor," said Evans, "how much would you get paid for an operation like this back in America?" "About five hundred dollars," came the reply.

[1] Louis H. Evans, *Youth Seeks a Master* (Fleming H. Revell Company, New York), pp. 80-81

"It was a complicated case." "How much will you get here?" The surgeon turned and looked at the poor Korean woman who had been wheeled into the operating room clutching only a copper coin and begging him in Christ's name to give her back life. Then he said, with tears welling up in his fine eyes, "For this I will get her gratitude and my Master's smile. But that, sir, is worth more than all the praise and money that the world can give."

It worries me when I begin drifting away from the realities of the Faith. I have a sense of loneliness, of being cut loose from people whom I admire the most, the servants of Christ in my own generation, and the saints who worship God before his throne in heaven. I cannot be indifferent to the fruits of the Holy Spirit in the lives of good men, the tradition of unselfish devotion and service reaching from the Cross of Christ down through the centuries into the Churches of our own day. It is precisely this sense of fellowship with the great Christians that encourages me and anchors me to the Faith. Dr. Dale of Birmingham once wrote by way of comparison : "If I were the only person who saw the sun rise this morning, then I might doubt my experience and call myself the victim of an illusion. But if I hear that many people in different countries and of varied intellectual powers have seen the same thing, and if I am told that men and women have laid down their lives rather than deny its reality, then my doubt vanishes and I become sure of myself."

In *The Pilgrim's Progress* (not "Regress" this time, but "Progress") the Interpreter shows Christian a fire burning against a wall. Nearby stands a man who keeps pouring water on the fire, but however much he pours, he fails to extinguish it. Then the Interpreter takes Christian behind the wall where he discovers another man, hidden from view, who continually pours oil on the fire, so that it burns higher and hotter. The Interpreter explains this acted parable : the Devil would quench our faith, but Christ with the oil of grace maintains the work already begun in our hearts. Christ redeemed us, and therefore Christ accepts responsibility for us. We may relax our grip on him, but he does not relax his grip on us. None of us need drift away from reality, for when we have thrown out those anchors of the soul, we shall discover the most marvellous truth that the love which first claimed us will not let us go and that Christ also has lines which he throws out to secure us and hold us to reality.

You remember I said that Dr. Forster painted two portraits and that they hang side by side in the Canadian School of Missions. The second painting bears the title "Faith", and it shows the young art student no longer surrounded by symbols, but dressed in a pure white robe and looking upwards with a serene expression on her beautiful face. Miss Smart found what she had lost; she rediscovered her faith; by the grace of God she stopped drifting and was brought back again to the eternally real. That was the climax of her spiritual biography, and by the grace of God it can be yours.

20

REFUSING TO GROW UP

"Therefore let us leave the elementary doctrines of Christ and go on to maturity . . ."

(Hebrews 6:1)

THE PICTURE is that of a university. We are to think of ourselves, once we have accepted the Lordship of Jesus Christ, as enrolled in the Christian school of life, members of the apostolic community, students of the Master of Life. The Christian School differs from other schools in this respect—that it never issues diplomas; on this side of eternity, at least, one never reaches a point where he exhausts the curriculum and has nothing more to learn. Of course, there are those who do think of themselves as alumni and retain only an emotional attachment to the Christian School, supporting its drives for funds and returning for an occasional reunion, especially at Easter, when the present-day student body puts on a good show to prove that there is still some life left in the old institution. But these honorary members have never really finished their course; they have merely dropped out as sophomores, because from the Christian School there is no earthly graduation. To enroll at all is to enroll for life.

An important principle governs the life of a university, the principle of academic progress. On various subjects one may take introductory courses, but having laid the foundations of knowledge, he is then expected to build on them, proceeding to more advanced courses and developing proficiency in particular fields. Should he qualify for a Bachelor's Degree, he does not then make a career of acquiring Bachelor's Degrees, but moves on to the Master's status, then to the doctorate and even post-doctoral study. In time he will become a teacher. In Canada I asked the President of a great university, "How long have you been here?" He replied, "Forty years. I started as an undergraduate, then did post-graduate work, became a lecturer, an assistant, associate and full professor, a dean, and finally President."

The writer of the Epistle to the Hebrews was very certain that this principle of academic growth should govern the Christian life. "Therefore let us leave the elementary doctrines of Christ and go on to maturity. . . ." He has already warned his readers of the danger of drifting away from the faith. Now he warns them of another danger, that of standing still in the faith, of falling over sideways because they fail to move ahead. Sharply he reprimands them, tells them that as second-generation Christians they should have achieved some degree of proficiency in the new religion and have reached a point where they could accept responsibility for the younger Christians coming along. By now they should be teachers, schooled in advanced Christianity. Instead they themselves seem to require instruction in the A.B.C.s of religious knowledge and experience. They are like children still living on a nursery diet in the Church. They have never gone beyond the introductory courses of Christianity.

The author of Hebrews brings us face to face with a problem which haunts the Church in every generation, which plagues the ministry and frustrates our work as we seek to interpret the Word of God and care for the souls of our people and guide the Church in its witness before the world. It is the problem of Christians who refuse to grow up.

There are Christians who refuse to grow up *spiritually*. Such people would not deny our Lord's injunction to Nicodemus; they believe implicitly, almost too implicitly, that "unless a man be born again, he cannot see the Kingdom of God". They themselves may have had such a conversion experience which made them new creatures in Christ. Very definitely, decisively and dramatically they have enrolled as freshmen in the Christian school of life, but for some reason they want to remain freshmen. Having been born a second time, they expect to go on being born a third time and a fourth and a fifth, saved, converted and redeemed *ad infinitum.* Such people will readily enough shirk their responsibility in the life and work of the Church, but let some colourful evangelist come to the city, and they sit conspicuously in the front row ready to leap to their feet the moment he extends his altar call. It would be interesting to analyse the case histories of converts at an evangelistic mission to discover how many have made "decisions" before and will probably make them again. Do they experience an emotional jag in this repeated revivalism, or do they simply refuse to grow up? They are like children going through their birth pangs over and over again, everlastingly suckled on milk, content with a diet of pablum and never tasting the solid food of Christian maturity.

There are Christians who refuse to grow up *intellectually.* At their mother's knee and in Sunday School they acquired a certain religious knowledge, and this elementary knowledge has served them ever since. They have never added to it or improved upon it. In mechanical matters, in their vocations, in managing a home and in handling their finances they have achieved a mature proficiency, but today, well past middle-age, they think of God and his purpose and judgment and love and activity exactly as they did when they were children. They know that great advances have been made in Biblical scholarship and theological thought over the past fifty years, but they wave them aside and mutter something about being satisfied with the simple Gospel (as though the mystery of God become man could ever be called simple). Such people would be appalled at a physician who refused to prescribe new drugs or a surgeon who would not authorize new anaesthetics on the ground that what was good enough in medicine fifty years ago is good enough today. Yet they make exactly that demand on the pulpit. The preacher whom they flock to hear is the simple story-teller who dispenses homiletic pap instead of the solid food of God's Word. It is one of the tragedies of the Church that preachers make so little effort to teach their congregations new knowledge, new truth, new approaches and new thought —and this because they feel intimidated by the lethargy of lazy minds and the embattled prejudice of shut minds.

Many a minister in his passion to be popular has deserved
the rebuke of an old sermon-taster who said, "That fellow's
education was certainly a waste of time!"

There are Christians who refuse to grow up *morally*.
Even outside the Church we talk of mature and immature
behaviour. You hear it said of a person, "He is just an over-
grown boy!" or "Why doesn't he act his age?" We mean
that though physically he is an adult, a man with a responsible position and a family, yet emotionally he reacts to some
situations like a child, blowing tin horns at a business con-
vention and sulking in a corner when he fails to get his own
way. We are all sinners to begin with. None of us become
saints overnight, and perhaps our characters in the early
stage of Christian growth will show little likeness to him
whom we profess to serve and obey. We expect, however,
that a person who enrolls in the school of Christ will, as he
grows older, reflect the character of Christ more and more.
All the time he will be ridding himself of old faults and acquiring new virtues. His life will grow more lovely, more
strong and more fine; it will radiate a new patience, a new
serenity, a new unselfishness, a new nobility. Nothing does
more to bring the Church into disrepute than a case of
arrested moral development, the sight of some respected and
influential member of long standing disgracing himself in the
community or fomenting congregational strife with all the
bad-tempered petulance of a Sunday School child. Many a
minister has been driven to a sense of failure by the conduct
of people who refused to act like mature Christians. "What
am I doing here?" the man of God exclaims to his wife.
"What have I been preaching about all these years?"

Let us ask where the difficulty lies. Why do many Christians refuse to advance beyond the first principles of Christian experience and become teachers in the Christian school
of life? Perhaps we can find a clue in the passing remark of
an Oxford theologian whom I came to know a few years ago
while doing post-graduate study at that university. He expressed interest that I had taken time out of my ministry
to renew contact with theological thought, but he said, "I
hope you have not come here simply to take a refresher

course. I deplore this habit of professional men to be ever-lastingly attending lectures and re-schooling themselves in the A.B.C.s of their vocation. Such people," he said, "refuse to grow up. They refuse to take their place as mature men in an adult world." He went on to say, in effect, that a man who would grow in scholarship must get beyond the place where he has constantly to be on the receiving end. He must reach a point where he is prepared to think and to work independently and make his own distinctive contribution to the body of knowledge.

Here, indeed, is the essence of any kind of maturity, the goal of any wise parent as he guides his son through infancy, childhood and adolescence. His object is to make himself as a parent increasingly unnecessary to the boy, get him to stand on his own feet and reach a point where he can think for himself, make his own decisions and accept responsibility. To grow up in an academic community means that having mastered Grade Nine, you advance to the more concentrated work of Grade Ten, and from Secondary School you pro-ceed to university with its absence of spoon-feeding and its sterner discipline of independent study. What does it mean to grow up in the Christian community? It means that you will come down from the spectator's balcony and get into the arena of the Christian struggle. It means that you will carry your share of the Church's life and work; you will accept your responsibility for the Church's witness; you will make your contribution to the Church's ongoing mission. It takes courage to grow up as a Christian, and many Chris-tians do not possess courage. They find it so much easier to let others do the thinking and make the decisions and carry the burdens; as for themselves they will live like Peter Pan in a Never-Never Land of childish fantasy.

One of the pew stewards in a large downtown church observed a man standing at the entrance of the church and apparently participating in the service of worship. He had seen this man on several Sundays and had noticed that he invariably took up the same position—a regular worshipper, but never advancing beyond the vestibule into the main body of the church. In Christian friendliness the sidesman approached him and said kindly, "Let me show you to a seat." Whereupon the stranger turned tail, walked out of the building and never came back again. Obviously he did not want to be welcomed or drawn into the Christian fellowship; he wanted to be in the Church but not of it, an unidentified, anonymous fugitive on the Church's fringe. Why do many potential Christians shyly keep the Church at arm's length, drop in for worship occasionally, but walk away quickly when you approach them and suggest that they integrate themselves into the Church's life? Are they afraid of what it would involve to become identified formally and publicly with the visible fellowship of Christians; afraid of what it might cost in convenience, comfort and character; afraid that their friends outside the Church will point an accusing finger at them and judge them by a higher standard than they were willing to apply to themselves? They are like school children who choose to remain permanently in kindergarten, playing with blocks and crayons, while other pupils advance to the maturing disciplines of reading and arithmetic. None of us can pretend to have "arrived" in the Christian life by committing ourselves in the vows of Church membership to work actively for the Church's witness and mission, but we do believe that we have set our feet in the Way of Christ and declared our intention, with the help of God's Holy Spirit, to grow in that Way.

How shall we interpret the message of our Lord save as a summons to Christian maturity? Jesus loved children. He called them to himself, took them up in his arms, fondled them on his knee and told them stories. Once he set a child in the midst of his disciples and said, "Except you humble yourself as this little child, you will not enter the Kingdom of God." There was nothing childish about his teaching, however; it called men to a new maturity of thought and behaviour. Jesus made it very clear that whoever would be his disciple must advance beyond the elementary standards of civilized decency and subject himself to the sublime rule of the Kingdom. "For I tell you that unless your righteousness exceeds that of the Scribes and Pharisees, unless it goes beyond the first principles, the basic rudiments of

morality—you will never enter the Kingdom of heaven."
Did the law prohibit murder? "I say to you that every one
who is angry with his brother shall be liable to judgment."
Did the law forbid adultery? "I say to you that every one
who looks at a woman lustfully has already committed
adultery with her in his heart." Did the law permit divorce?
"I say to you, whom God hath joined together let not man
put asunder." Did the law condone revenge? "I say to you,
love your enemies and pray for those who persecute you."

In a book bearing this very title, John Wick Bowman calls
Christianity *The Religion of Maturity*.[1] He traces the religion
of the Old Testament through its various expressions in
priesthood, prophecy and apocalypse and presents the thesis
that this religion of altar, book and throne reaches its
maturing process in the revelation of God in Jesus Christ.
In Jesus the religion of the Jews achieved fulfilment, it grew
up; but growing up was precisely what many Jews did not
have the courage to do. They resisted God's process of
maturity, they rejected it, they ridiculed it, and at last in
blind fury they nailed it to a cross. They refused to grow up
and therefore doomed themselves to such elementary knowledge and experience of God as they already possessed, while
followers of the Risen Christ moved onward and upward
to maturity.

The whole story of Christianity has been a story of
growth into maturity. Like a student who advances to higher
and higher degrees, so the Church has followed its course
through history, sometimes moving steadily forward, then
receding, often remaining for centuries in a particular stage
of development, then surging upward suddenly into a period
of accelerated and pronounced growth. In its earliest years
came the challenge of the Gentiles, and the Church had to
break with the ritual requirements of the Jewish Law and
make the decision whereby Christianity could become a
religion for all peoples. In the sixteenth century came the
challenge of the Renaissance, the resurgence of pure learning
and the beginnings of invention and discovery, an awakening
of independent thought in the minds of men which, to some

[1] Abingdon-Cokesbury Press (New York—Nashville 1948)

extent, was answered by the Protestant Reformation. In our day has come the challenge of global revolutions, backward nations achieving the sense of selfhood, totalitarian régimes bidding for world domination, and scientific miracles binding the human race to a common destiny. Can it not be said that the modern missionary movement and the ecumenical movement are, in part, an answer to this challenge? At each decisive period in history the Church seems to have gathered its strength and moved upward to a new stage of maturity in thought and witness, but each time, of course, there have been reactionaries, Christian people who fought against the maturing process, who refused to go along with it, and, as a consequence, were left behind.

Only a mature Christianity can save an immature civilization. A magazine article asks us to picture an eighteen-month-old infant suddenly grown, within a month or two, to his full physical stature. Instead of measuring thirty-one inches and weighing twenty-five pounds, he now stands six feet and weighs one hundred and ninety. Suppose also that during this month or two of rapid physical growth, his intellect has developed proportionately and he has even attended university and been granted a degree. In other respects, however, he has not developed. He still slobbers and drools, still bellows when he is hungry, still goes into a temper tantrum at the least frustration. He understands nothing of how other people feel. He responds only to those who do things for him. He becomes sullen and suspicious. He has no real affection or loyalty. But with his superior physique and intellect he has enough strength and cunning to manipulate others to do his will, regardless of what is just or socially enlightened. It is a parable of our civilization, phenomenally advanced physically and intellectually, but woefully immature morally and spiritually. Modern man resembles a little monster who goes about kicking his dark-skinned brother in the face, monopolizing the food and the beds while other members of the family go hungry and sleep on the floor, and inventing dangerous explosives in the basement with which he threatens to blow up the whole house, including himself, if he does not get his own way. Consider this remarkable fact about man: that while he has made progress, he himself is not progressive. Through all the revolutions wrought by his inventive genius man remains basically the same, living in the space age as irrationally, as selfishly, as childishly, as he did in the dark ages. The human race has simply refused to grow up.

How often we have repeated that stirring prayer of Walter Rauschenbusch—"O God, we pray for thy Church, which is set today amid the perplexities of a changing order, and face to face with a great new task. . . ." The late Albert Camus, by no stretch of the imagination a Christian believer, declared cynically when he accepted the Nobel Prize that whereas once we tried to improve civilization, now it has become our concern to prevent civilization from being blown to bits. That is the Church's great new task in this mid-twentieth century—to hold the world together; and to accomplish that miracle, it will require a more mature Christianity than the world has thus far seen. A Church which in its treatment of coloured peoples lags behind the secular spheres of entertainment and sport will have nothing to teach the world in mitigating its racial dilemmas. A Church which has not yet caught up to the labour unions in the struggle for social justice will have little effect in promoting a more responsible society. A Church which sustains the oldest, most powerful and most entrenched dictatorship in the world will beat like a feather on the iron tyranny of modern totalitarian systems. A Church which lives in the past and refuses to rethink its theology will be a feeble voice in a world where scientific miracles have revolutionized the thoughts of men. A Church whose member bodies cannot be reconciled to one another will appear ridiculous as it attempts to reconcile the world to God. A Church which ignores the human situation and takes refuge in subjective evangelicalism, sterile sacramentalism and stuffy ecclesiasticism will not have power to arrest the human race in its downward descent to hell. Too often the Church gives the impression of a boy trying to do a man's job. Hold civilization together? Not by Christians who refuse to grow up.

"Therefore let us leave the elementary doctrines of Christ and go on to maturity...." The picture is that of a university. What a thrilling experience for any youth to leave home and go to college and begin preparation for his life's work, a thrill surpassed only by the day when that college confers a degree on him and declares him qualified to practise medicine or teach in a school or engage in some other profession. But neither entrance nor graduation is of first importance. What really matters is what that boy learns during his university career, the knowledge he acquires, the maturing of his mind. So in the Christian school of life we must not fix all our emphasis upon its beginning and ending, because both are contingent upon what happens in between. Either we must grow in the faith, leave the elementary doctrines of Christ and go on to maturity, or we shall fall away from the faith altogether; we shall cancel our conversion and certainly never qualify for graduation. But growth, no less than salvation and eternal life, comes to us as a gift of God. Christ, who started us on our course and who receives us at the end, will accompany us and help us through all the years of study; he will lead us onward and upward to new and higher stages of maturity as we turn to him in faith and obedience.

21

THE PILGRIM VIEW OF LIFE

". . . having acknowledged that they were strangers and
exiles on the earth."

(Hebrews 11 : 13)

PREACHING AT a funeral service a minister made the statement, "My friends, we are living for two worlds." He was
challenged afterwards by a successful businessman who
said, "We are living for one world and one only. We do not
know of any other world than this one." The minister thought
a moment and then asked, "If you did believe in another
world, would it make any difference to you?" The reply came
without hesitation, "Of course it would. If I had the slightest suspicion that we are really living for any other world
than this, I should change every major business policy I have
before night."

We should all make some radical changes in our affairs
if once we took seriously the teaching of the New Testament.
Never does the Bible regard this world as life's final destination. By the grace of God we have been born and permitted to dwell here for a season, but nature itself fixes
limits to the time of our sojourn. Repeatedly the Bible pictures life as a pilgrimage, a journey through time and space
which allows nothing more than brief resting-places along
the way. Every passing day completes a stage of the journey.

The author of the Epistle to the Hebrews employs some
very suggestive words to emphasize this journey-concept of
life. Writing of Israel's patriarchs, he calls them "strangers
and exiles", terms which in the ancient world were regarded with contempt, because they denoted what we understand as "refugees". Again he calls them "resident aliens",
a class of people who ranked little higher than slaves in the

social scale; the resident alien was an outsider, a man who became a member of the community on sufferance and by payment of an alien tax. Again he uses a word that means "wanderer", a traveller living in temporary lodgings, a man with "no fixed abode" in a country where life has sent him. All their lives the patriarchs lived as strangers in a strange land, men with no settled place that they could call "home". To the end of their days they were pilgrims, travelling from one place to another, never striking roots, but always on the move.

According to the writer of Hebrews this picture of the sojourner, the stranger, the foreigner, the pilgrim, is an accurate picture of the Christian life. He has already warned the little community of Christians in Rome that they face two dangers—drifting away from the faith and failing to mature in the faith. Now he warns them of the great peril of losing their sense of direction in the faith (what the theologians call "the eschatological perspective of the faith"), the sense of where they are going, or the sense that they are going anywhere at all. He admonishes them to be aware that as Christians they are living for two worlds. Always their life in the Christian community must be dominated by the impermanence of this world and by the Ultimate End to which God is leading them. Without this awareness their faith cannot possibly survive; with it they can withstand the mightiest onslaughts of hell. It is a timely word of God to our situation. I can think of no dimension that we need more urgently to recover in our thinking today than the concept of life as a pilgrimage, a journey from eternity through time to eternity.

I

If we take seriously the pilgrim view of life, we shall place a lower premium on material security. That would indeed make a radical change in our thinking because, like most of our contemporaries, we worship security; we make it a god; upon its altar we sacrifice many values—initiative, freedom, adventure, even our ideals. Among intellectuals it has become fashionable to sneer at security, to talk of it as an illusion and to insist that there are values in life more precious than physical safety and material comfort. It is not the unworthiness or illusoriness of security that we need to emphasize, however, but its impermanence, the obvious truth that what we possess in this world belongs to us only for a season and that even the most impregnable fortress can afford only a night's lodging to the pilgrim on his way to eternity.

The contrast is exactly that between a temporary posting in a foreign country and taking out citizenship in that country. As a citizen you have a sense of permanence; you belong there, you dig in, you establish a home and ensconce yourself in the life of the community. As a traveller you have no such sense of belonging. You may enjoy the foreign land and speak its language, make friends and work there for a season, but never do you feel tempted to settle down and "go native". You don't purchase a house, you rent one. You may not even unpack thoroughly, because all the time you know that the supreme fact dominating all your possessions and relationships in that country is that you will eventually have to leave them. It recalls an unwritten saying of Jesus, "The world is a bridge. The wise man will pass over it, but he will not build his house upon it."

The Christians in Rome needed desperately to learn this lesson. Their security had been taken away from them. Because they had accepted the Lordship of Jesus Christ and renounced the lordship of Caesar, they were socially ostracized, politically disenfranchised, ecclesiastically scorned and economically impoverished. Already they had suffered persecution and would probably do so again; daily they lived under the shadow of that great world building, the Colosseum, where hungry lions tore limb from limb the bodies of traitors to the state. They were like any group of Christians behind the Iron Curtain today, penalized in countless subtle ways and never knowing when the hand on the shoulder might fall. How they envied the security of their pagan compatriots! How tempted they were to mortgage their souls, take the cash and let the credit go, settle for what the world had to offer and sacrifice that dubious quality of life called eternal.

The author of Hebrews does not scold them, he does not disparage the security for which they long, but he does urge upon them a view of life that sets security in its right perspective—as something which is good but not ultimately good, because it is stationary; it cannot accompany the pilgrim on his journey; it must eventually be left behind.

This is not the whole truth about life. It is, however, a tremendously important truth which would certainly change our thinking if ever we attempted to live on the basis of it. Would a man expend so much of his energy in trying to make money if ever he reckoned seriously with the truth that pounds and dollars are not negotiable in heaven? Would a woman invest so much of her personality in creating a pretentious home if she anticipated the order to move out of that home and live elsewhere? Would many of us allow our decisions to be determined by material factors if we could see how relatively unimportant those factors are in the total scheme of life? It all adds up to our Lord's parable of the Rich Fool. He thought himself secure in the possession of big barns, but there are no big barns if you plan to store a human soul in them. If that is what you plan, then the barns become smaller and smaller and the foolishness grows larger and larger until nothing is left but heaven's thunderous comment on the vast absurdity of it all, "Thou fool, this night thy soul shall be required of thee. Then whose shall those things be which thou hast provided?"

II

If we take seriously the pilgrim view of life, we shall no longer attach ultimate importance to relative values. At this point the writer of Hebrews speaks more directly to the Church than to the individual, because the danger that confronts the Church in any age is that it will lose sight of its nature as the pilgrim people of God and will settle down as a fixed, immovable community, seeking its reasons for existence in those things which are derivative and secondary.

This had happened to the Church of the Old Covenant. After Moses led the children of Israel out of Egypt into the wilderness, he gave them a "tent" or "tabernacle" as the place of God's presence. It was the first Church building ever constructed, and its flimsy, mobile character symbolized God's dealings with his people, his plan to uproot them periodically and lead them onward to new revelations of himself. The tent was brought into Canaan, and for three hundred years it stood as a type or figure of God's never-ceasing, never-halted appointments for his people's salvation. In the prosperous days of the Monarchy Israel desired a more stable dwelling for the Most High, and Solomon built a temple, but the point is that the temple was not intended, any more than the Tabernacle, to become a permanent institution, halting the advance of the Divine plan for the people of God. The tragedy of the Old Israel, as Stephen thundered forth in his great apology, was that this very thing had happened. The Jews had identified their salvation with earthly securities and fixtures. They were too blind to see that with the coming of Jesus the hour had struck for moving on from the temple. Indeed, because Christ threatened the temple, they crucified him, and in so doing removed themselves from the Divine purpose.

The Church of the Middle Ages identified salvation with earthly securities and fixtures. Distinguished theologians from Augustine to Bossuet presented impressive arguments to support the claim that in the Church of Rome, its theology, institutions and sacramental system, the Word of God had found final form, and that while that Word allowed of interpretation, yet even God himself would never add to it or take away from it. To put it more crudely, the Church of Rome had shut God up in a box and worshipped that box instead of worshipping God. Against this frank idolatry the Reformers of the sixteenth century protested, but in so doing they did not intend that God should simply be transplanted to another fixed, immovable, idolized box. As Paul Tillich defines it, "The Protestant principle, in name derived from the protests of the 'Protestants' against the decisions of the Catholic majority, contains the Divine and human protest against any absolute claim made for a relative reality, even if this claim is made by a Protestant Church."

In a series of lectures delivered at Oxford University, the General Secretary of the World Council of Churches said,

> "To build the Church is not to build up a solid institution which is wholly at home in the world and uses the methods of the world. It is rather to organize a band of pilgrims who are on the way to a new and better country and who must therefore not adapt themselves to their temporary surroundings."[1]

How entirely appropriate, coming from a leader of the ecumenical movement; because there will be no real progress in the ecumenical movement, no real coming together of the Churches until the Churches break away from their pre-Reformation idolatries, from giving to an episcopal system, or a democratic process, or a form of liturgy, or a collection of writings, or a body of doctrine, or a subjective experience, the worship and obedience due only to Christ. If the Church could once re-awaken to its essential nature as the pilgrim people of God, then it would realize that all these things are derivative and secondary; important, but of relative importance. They constitute only a night's lodging on the way to the homeland and the Church should always be ready at God's command to move on and leave any one of them behind.

III

If we take seriously the pilgrim view of life, we shall always be ready for bold experiments and courageous advance. The picture of the patriarchs as itinerant tent-dwellers should be appealing in these days when camping has become a hobby no longer restricted to Boy Scouts. A friend of mine is always urging me to try it some summer vacation. The very thought makes me itch; but it does sound exciting to hear him tell of how he and his family set out with absolute freedom for the wide open spaces. After driving all day, they stop at nightfall by the shores of some beautiful lake where it takes his youngsters about fifteen minutes to

[1] W. A. Visser 't Hooft, .The Renewal of the Church (S.C.M. Press, London 1956)

pitch camp; and the next morning, after another fifteen minutes to load the car, they are off again. The advantage, apparently, is that they travel light and are never tied down to any one location. They can enjoy some scenic surroundings for a few days, and when the urge takes them, they can move on with a minimum of inconvenience.

It is a picture of the Christian life which is essentially an adventurous life, almost a reckless life in its readiness for bold experiments and courageous advance. The Christian differs from other men in this respect, that while they act from motives of caution and prudence, the Christian acts from faith which, as *Hebrews* defines it, is "the assurance of things hoped for, the conviction of things not seen". Faith is supremely the willingness to take risks for God; unless it takes risks it is not faith. As a type and figure of faith, the author of Hebrews points to Abraham who, in answer to God's call, gathered his whole family and left the lush security of Ur of the Chaldees and "went out, not knowing whither he went". By faith Abraham became a tent-dweller, a pilgrim, never building a permanent home on this earth, but always ready to pull up stakes at a moment's notice and move onward in response to the great new initiatives of God.

In one of his books Bishop Lesslie Newbigin describes the negotiations which led to the formation of the Church of South India. He himself had a share in this ecumenical experiment, and he tells of how things were frequently held up by cautious and prudent people who wanted to know just where each step was leading them and what would happen if they made this or that decision. At length the Chairman reminded them that they had better try to approach the matter as Christians, because a Christian is a man who must be ready to follow God with no guarantee of where he is going. The real peril facing the Church in South India, or anywhere else, is not that it will make the wrong decisions, but that it will refuse to make decisions at all and will be governed by the counsel of timorous, stubborn, worldly, reactionary men. Bishop Newbigin makes it clear that the Church of South India has no thought of resting on its achievements; it does not pretend to have arrived, but it does claim to be on the right road. The Church is the pilgrim people of God; it can never be defined in terms of what it now is, but only in terms of the End towards which God is leading it; and the Church which is true to its own nature will always be ready, under the impulse of God's Holy Spirit, for bold experiments and courageous advance.

The late George Bernard Shaw neither understood nor sympathized with the witness and mission of the Church, but, like many another observer from the street, he could recognize shallowness and infidelity when he saw it. His play, *Heartbreak House*, which was revived on Broadway two years ago, has a warning for the Church no less valid today than when Shaw wrote it. The action takes place toward the close of World War I, and it ends with the bombing raids—a timely situation that takes on greater urgency now that bombs have grown bigger than they were in 1917. When the planes roar over England dropping explosives and lighting up the sky, the hero of the play, Captain Shotover, climbs the mast of his ship-house to see where the destruction falls. "The Church is on the rocks," he cries, "I told them it would be unless it headed for God's open sea!"

IV

If we take seriously the pilgrim view of life, we shall travel with our eyes focused on the final destination. Somebody asked a man who lived in the London suburb of Battersea where he intended going for his summer holidays. He replied, "To Battersea". Then he hastened to add, "I shall go by way of the southern coast of France and Italy, but my final destination will be Battersea." Every journey reaches its climax on the day we return home. What gives meaning to our travel through foreign lands is the constant thought that we have a home to return to, and that love and warmth and familiar surroundings await us at the end of the journey. We enjoy our travels abroad, but as the days pass we think more and more of home and we keep in touch with home and we look forward to returning home. So the author of

Hebrews could say of the patriarchs that "people who speak thus make it clear that they are seeking a homeland". Their bodies wandered through the earth, but their souls were ever at home with God; they were strangers and exiles, not despising the environment in which they lived, but travelling through it with their gaze fixed on the final destination of heaven.

This concept of life as a journey should make a tremendous difference in our attitude towards old age and death. By now the world has forgotten Caryl Chessman, but a year or so ago many of us felt a sense of revulsion at the obsolescence of a law which could execute even a guilty man after torturing his soul for twelve years. With full recognition of his criminal record, we somehow admired the grim tenacity with which this condemned man clung to life, and secretly we hoped that he would cheat the gas chamber again and go on cheating it. But the tragedy of Caryl Chessman is not that he lost his battle to live; rather that he died with an expression of utter hopelessness on his lips—"Nothing beyond death!" he declared—so that even had he been reprieved, his essential situation would have remained unchanged. That is the tragedy of so many lives these days, of people who frantically try to disguise the process of growing old and who pathetically welcome every new miracle drug, which, though it may alter the immediate situation and prolong life for another year or two, leaves the essential situation unchanged.

We can thank God that we are Christians. Thank God that we see ourselves as pilgrims travelling through time to eternity and that each passing day brings us closer to our final destination. What a difference when we can see that destination! Imagine a man travelling through the darkness who comes to the edge of a frozen pond. Confused, bewildered and not at all sure of where he is going, he starts out across the ice. After he has gone a little way in the darkness, he slips and hurts himself. Uncertain that there is anything but darkness and cold and more slipperiness ahead of him, he curses the whole situation and exclaims, "Oh, what's the use!" In contrast, imagine another man travelling the same way through the darkness who comes to the edge of the pond and, without too much indecision, starts across because he can see a light on the far shore. He, too, falls on the ice and hurts himself. He, too, is tempted to curse the darkness. But because he sees the light he struggles on, knowing that warmth and love await him at the end of his journey. That is a picture of the Christian life, no easier than any other life, a more anguished life perhaps, because it brings us into closer touch with reality. Many times we have it on our tongue to say, "What's the use!" but we do not say it; we struggle onwards, because through all the darkness we can see a light that marks the end of our journey, and that light beckons us towards home.

From the inaugural assembly of the World Council of Churches at Amsterdam in 1948 came this message.

> "There is a Word from God to this world. It states that the world is in the hands of the living God whose will for it is wholly good; that in Jesus Christ, his Incarnate Word, who lived and died and rose from the dead, God has broken the power of evil once for all, and opened for everyone the gate of freedom and joy in the Holy Spirit . . . and that the end of history will be the triumph of his Kingdom. . . ."

There is the dimension that needs desperately to be recovered in the thinking of Christian people if we would preserve our faith strong and serene in a day when everything in life and the world seems to intimidate it. Like the patriarchs of Israel we must learn to look beyond the failures and frustrations of the world in which we live, and focus our vision on that Ultimate End towards which God has ever been seeking to lead and impel his people. In this world we do seem to have made a sorry mess of things, but let us not lose heart, for when we have done our best, we are still living for two worlds. We are a pilgrim people travelling through time to eternity, and beyond all the wrecks of history is the goal of history, our homeland, the blessed Kingdom of God.